PRAISE FOR LIFE RE-SCRIPTED

"A few things that struck me about Zeph's book. First it's super easy to read. Second is I related to it so darn much because I too have had struggles in life that I have had to overcome, so I felt connected in a unique way. Finally was the way Zeph wraps it all into a wicked simple rule called the 'Struggle to Hustle Golden Ratio'. Thanks Zeph for showing the courage to put your story out into the world and sharing it with us."

–Rick Martinez, Founder and CEO BizAcademyOnline.com

"Having personally witnessed Zephan grow from a 9-5 tech guru into the entrepreneur that he is today is proof enough that anyone can do this. But it isn't in his nature to keep his strategies all to himself which is exactly why he wrote Life Re-Scripted – to share his message with the world. Zephan has been instrumental in supporting me and my vision to bring my business to the next level. In this book, you'll find a blueprint for not only pinpointing where you are now in life but you will also walk away with the ability to reorient the compass and point to your true purpose. This is more than a book you should read. It's your true road map to success"

– Judy Hoberman, President, Selling In A Skirt

"Are you directing your own life -- or just going through the motions in someone else's script? Zephan masterfully shows you how to ask the tough questions and take control of your own destiny to live a life of greater purpose, meaning, and fulfillment."

–Nick Loper, Chief Side Hustler, Side Hustle Nation

"In Life Re-Scripted, Zephan has an extraordinary amount to teach you. This is a front-row seat to his amazing journey of transformation from a burnt-out, 9-to-5 corporate employee to highly successful business owner with an invite to work at the White House — all by age 26. Beyond providing inspiration and insight, Zephan has creatively packaged up his experiences into bite-sized actionable tips that every person on a life-long quest of personal development needs to read. If you've ever wished you could re-write your own story, or even simply break free from life's inertia, this is a must-read!"

–Angelique Rewers, CEO and Founder, The Corporate Agent

"Life Re-Scripted is packed full of relatable and straightforward advice for purpose-seekers who are looking for the next big breakthrough or the next step to take in life. Zephan's book contains the perfect combination of real life examples and inspiration for millennials. It will leave you motivated to change your life immediately."

–Tim Paige, Conversion Educator, LeadPages

"If you're looking to find your purpose and live a happier life, then 'Life Re-scripted' is a must read for you! Through his stories and purpose-building tips, Zephan gives you everything you need to know to overcome what's holding you back and live a more meaningful life."

*–Michelle Prince, Zig Ziglar Motivational Speaker, Best-Selling Author
& Self-Publishing Expert, www.MichellePrince.com*

"In Life Re-Scripted, Zephan takes you step- by- step through how to remake the movie of your life, from Choosing Your Showtime to The Closing Credits. This is your guide to a better, more meaningful life, one full of fun, action and significance. You're going to be dead a longtime, so why not let Zephan show you how to make the most of truly being ALIVE!"

–Mark Brodinsky, #1 Amazon-Best Selling Author, It Takes 2: Surviving Breast Cancer: A Spouse's Story and Huffington Post Blogger

"Zephan Blaxberg is not just another talking head pontificating about changing your life when you're stuck in a rut or facing a crisis. Wise beyond his years, he has lived it. His energy, positivity and solid approach to re-scripting your life is powerful - and more importantly, approachable. If you're looking for a new perspective, Zephan delivers."

–Maria Ross, Owner, Red Slice

"In Life Re-Scripted, Zephan covers some concepts which I believe are vital to expanding your reality and experience of life. He'll give you exercises designed to rapidly get you honest and clear about where you are in your life, how to begin to align with your purpose, and how to get unstuck when things get hard. Through it all, Zephan speaks with refreshing honesty about serious challenges he's faced and overcome on his journey to health and success as a young entrepreneur. If you're feeling stuck in your life, unhappy with the results you've generated so far as a result of your mindset and action, I recommend you read Life Re-Scripted and use the exercises to start the process of reinvention that needs to happen for you to move forward in a direction that's in line with your true desires and purpose. In just a few short hours you could find yourself with a whole new perspective on your life and what you need to do next."

–Simon Smart, Founder, Warrior Protocol

"Being stuck between mediocrity and other people's expectations, can be a dangerous place; it can steal away potential and block worthy and worthwhile opportunities. In "Life Re-Scripted", Zephan engages and empowers us with tools and insight needed for reflection, consideration, implementation, and difference-making actions. Read this book and re-script life, based on your own terms."

– Joel Boggess, Life coach, #1 bestselling author, host of ReLaunch

"One of the toughest problems for millennials is determining what to do with your life when life really begins. Zephan masterfully explains lessons learned in his journey and how they apply to your story. Everyone wants to leave a legacy behind, the question becomes how significant will your story be? Will you re-script your life?"

– Arel Moodie, Best Selling Author of "Your Starting Point For Student Success" Founder of The College Success Program and The Art of Likability

"Few people talk about really finding your *why*. It is not a new subject. Zephan's book is not only about finding your why, but what you do after you find it. Unlike many new age touchy feely books about this subject I found Zephan's book to be refreshing and simple without taking anything away from this powerful message. And unlike many books on the subject I found a bigger message in Life Re-scripted. The message? Find what lesson you have mastered that you need to share with the world that will make the world a better place. And then Zephan helps you find the message that needs to be shared."

– Nile Nickel, CEO, LinkedinFocus.com and Host of the Social Media Business Hour

"We are all storytellers, and the greatest and most important story we can create and share is our own. Zephan Blaxberg's personal journey is an inspiring example of an amazing, positive "plot twist," and his book serves as a guide to those who are looking to create their own happy ending, and enjoy the adventure along the way. The book is a must-read for those looking to pursue their passion, and go from where they are to where they want to be."

– Lou Mongello, Author and Podcast Host, WDW Radio

"As a parent of three millennials, and having worked as a Relationship Coach for over 20 years, I've seen first hand how creating a life well lived creates stress, fear, and a sense of adventure. Life Re-Scripted offers an insider's view of what is possible when Passion, Purpose, and Perseverance are the companions in creating our life movie. Zephan opens up about obstacles and how our choices in facing them keep us on script or empower us to re-script our life. This book offers hope and practical help for a new generation who realized at a young age that life is not a dress rehearsal."

– Susie Miller, Author/Speaker/Better Relationships in 30 Days Coach,
www.susiemiller.com

LIFE
RE-SCRIPTED

Zephan Moses Blaxberg

Life Re-Scripted: Find Your Purpose and Design Your Dream Life Before The Curtains Close

Print ISBN-13: 978-0-9969599-0-2

eBook ISBN-13: 978-0-9969599-1-9

www.liferescriptedbook.com

Typesetting by Blush Book Design.

www.blushbookdesign.co.uk

STOP!
IMPORTANT:
Before You Continue...

Your Free Gift

As a way of saying thank you for purchasing this book, I'm offering you the following free book bonuses:

- The Life Re-Scripted Expert Interviews (over 40 entrepreneurs came together from all over the globe to share their secrets to creating a life and business on your own terms so that you can do it too)

- The Life Re-Scripted Transformation Challenge (to rewire your brain for maximum happiness and success so that you can discover your purpose and start living your dream life today)

- The Life Re-Scripted Inner Circle (a private community of entrepreneurs and life re-scripters from all over the globe who are living life on their own terms and want to support you because we all need someone to hold us accountable from time to time)

For exclusive access to these bonuses, go to

http://rescripted.life/bonus

For all the risks that you will take and all the mistakes that you will make, for this morning you were so fortunate as to arrive at this moment awake.

There were so many heroes in my life that inspired and motivated me to this point. Thanks for your support and for helping make this book possible!

- Allison E. Conway, Accountability Partner
- Ida Fia Svenningson, Amazing Cover Artist
- Carson Pohly, Masterful Web Manager
- Mara Glazer, Cut The Crap Coach
- Chandler Bolt, Self Publishing Coach
- Judy Hoberman, Entrepreneurial Mother
- Suzanne Kiewe, Biological Mother
- And so many more.

If I have left anyone else out from these acknowledgements, I will buy you a burrito to repent for my mistake.

Contents

Introduction   19

CHAPTER 1   **23**
Choose a Showtime   23
   A Re-script in My Life   28
   Life Re-Scripted Action Steps   33

CHAPTER 2   **35**
Concessions are Available in the Lobby   35
   Patience   38
   Passion   40
   Perseverance   41
   Life Re-Scripted Action Steps   47

CHAPTER 3   **48**
Take Your Seat   48
   The Blocked View   51
   The Sticky Floor   52
   Gratitude – the Best Seat in the House   54
   The Obnoxious Moviegoers   57
   Life Re-Scripted Action Steps   57

CHAPTER 4   **59**
Please Silence Your Cell Phones   59
   Turning Off Distractions   60
   The Inner Critic and the Inner Child   62
   Life Re-Scripted Action Steps   68

CHAPTER 5   **70**
The Following Preview Has Been Approved
for All Audiences   70
   Life Re-Scripted Action Steps   79

CHAPTER 6	**81**
Enjoy the Show	81
Tech Detox	83
Life Re-Scripted Action Steps	86
CHAPTER 7	**88**
The Opening Credits	88
Life-Casting Your Life	91
Life Re-Scripted Action Steps	94
CHPATER 8	**96**
Act One: The 5X Life Hack Rule	96
Struggle	98
Hustle	99
Editing	100
The Life-Scripting Exercise	101
Life Re-Scripted Action Steps	103
CHAPTER 9	**105**
Act Two: The Journey of the Protagonist, Part I	105
Climbing Out of the Cave	106
Finding Your Kryptonite	109
Creating a SMART Goal for Your Main Character	110
Train Your Mind & Body	112
Turning Your Enemies into Allies	114
Taking Action – Make the Change	117
Life Re-Scripted Action Steps	119
CHAPTER 10	**120**
Act Two: The Journey of the Protagonist, Part II	120
Life Re-Scripting Questions	123
Mental and Personal Development	*124*
Career and Business	*124*
Financial	*125*
Family	*126*
Social	*126*
Physical	*127*

Spiritual   *127*
Life Re-Scripted Action Steps   129

CHAPTER 11   **130**
The Bathroom Break   130
Life Re-Scripted Action Steps   136

CHAPTER 12   **137**
Act Three: The Plot Twist   137
The Circle of Purpose   139
Life Re-Scripted Action Steps   144

CHAPTER 13   **145**
And They Lived ____ Ever After   145
Life Re-Scripted Action Steps   148

CHAPTER 14   **150**
Closing Credits   150
Life Re-Scripted Action Steps   153

CHAPTER 15   **155**
Post Credits Scene   155

The Sequel   164

About The Author   171

Introduction

"At the end of our lives we all ask, 'Did I live? Did I love? Did I matter?'"

–Brendon Burchard

As we grow up, I believe that we are issued a script of how our lives should play out, including what we're "supposed" to do. But in a world that has uncountable resources readily available to give all of the answers, we're still stuck here wondering three things:

What is my purpose in life?

How can I be happy in the pursuit of this purpose?

How am I going to make a living out of my passions?

It's a travesty to have all the money you could need while missing the passionate drive to pull greatness out of yourself each and every day. We as a human race have settled for mediocrity, and there is an epidemic of ordinary people just like you and I who have sacrificed more than our fair share of happiness in the hunt for meaning and monetary compensation.

You aren't happy, you aren't filled with drive and you certainly don't know why you are doing the things you are doing over and over again.

This book will help you discover the answers to these age-old questions in a new and easy-to-accomplish approach. In fact, this concept is so simple that you could learn it in a weekend and take the fork in the road next week on a new path to greatness, a path well paved by happiness, aspirations and determination.

Are you feeling stuck? Are you still trying to figure out what it is that will spark the fire under you? The coals have been sitting there warm and dormant for years, waiting for a simple splash of lighter fluid or a dash of twigs to make the flames soar higher than ever. What if it were even easier to get the fire roaring again, like adding oxygen, which is an extremely abundant resource that is all around you?

Entrepreneurs, wantrepreneurs and corporate burnouts all over the world who struggle with finding happiness, freedom and, most importantly, their purpose, have already experienced great success by implementing the tips and tricks found in this helpful how-to guide.

One of my podcast listeners wrote to me, asking for help in getting her business launched on the side of her full-time job, in hopes of creating a freedom lifestyle for herself. At the cost of just nine dollars, she implemented one recommendation that I gave her, and within two weeks, she went from zero fans and potential clients to over fifty new members of her tribe. Each and every single one of them supported her mission. It was quite a noble mission, and with no expertise, she gathered complete strangers in one setting for her new business idea.

Lauren, an aspiring entrepreneur and student of mine from Atlanta, Georgia, says, "The best thing about the book is it can be read over a weekend, and by Monday, you are already on a path to creating big changes in your life. The surprising part is you'll be aligning yourself with your inner desires even if you don't know what they are at first."

There's Jen who left a job that was no longer serving her. The decision came from inside herself, and it only took about two hours to get there. It's not rocket science. I believe that we all know deep inside exactly where we want to go. It's just a matter of pulling out the right answers.

I promise that if you follow the how-to guide I've written for you here, you will get clear on your WHAT, and, more importantly, your WHY, five times faster than you would following your current trajectory. The purpose-building tips and tricks you're about to read have been proven to create positive, long lasting results. And I promise that you will create twice as much freedom in your life to do the things you really want to do without the fear of money or failure.

Don't be the person who misses out on living a meaningful life because you succumbed to your fears. Don't let the little voice in your head talk you out of living up to your fullest potential.

I know it may seem like a far off distant dream, but that is exactly where I was a few weeks before escaping the nine-to-five hustle and starting a business. It only took two weeks for me to make a drastic change for the better.

If you are the type of person who sits around reading self-help books, listening to motivational YouTube videos, hoping that one day, through osmosis, you will gain the courage to dive into the deep end, you will most certainly be in for a huge surprise, and not a good one. My wish for you is to be the person who loves every ounce of what life has to offer.

Be the kind of person that other people admire for their courage and success. Be the kind of person other people see and say, "I wish I could, but I could never do that."

Most importantly, be the kind of person who takes control over his or her life and starts living a life re-scripted.

Choose a Showtime

"Remembering that I'll be dead soon is the most important tool I've ever encountered to help me make the big choices in life. Because almost everything—all external expectations, all pride, all fear of embarrassment or failure—these things just fall away in the face of death, leaving only what is truly important."

–Steve Jobs

Throughout your life, you are going to find many stories. Some of them will be horror stories that keep you up at night, and if you're lucky, most will stick to the drama and comedy side. The first step in examining your life to determine what to do with it is to decide

LIFE
RE-SCRIPTED

what story you are going to follow. Chapter one is all about rebelling against the standards that have been set for you.

It all starts out with the movie. Ask Siri, the digital voice assistant on your Apple products, "What is the meaning of life?" and she'll respond in many ways. But I found it truly inspiring that her first response to me was, "A movie." I think we're on to something... After all, if Siri, says the meaning of life is a movie, then it must be true.

You walk up to the movie theater with its grand facade of flashing lights and neon signs, and it's just begging you to walk in and spend some time. But this theater is unlike any other, because this particular venue isn't showing the latest trilogy series or award-nominated thriller. No, this theater is a projector of life – with stories of love, sadness, triumph, loss, courage and every emotion in between. The theater's always open. In fact, the movie title never changes; it's just called *Life Re-Scripted* and it has a new showing every hour on the hour.

Want a matinee? No problem. Want to come in at 3 am? No problem. The movie is always being screened because it hasn't ended... yet. The bulbs on the projectors never overheat, the popcorn is always freshly buttered, and, I can assure you, the Super Freezee machine is always chilled and ready for use.

You step up to the glass doors, walk up to a booth, and behind it is a gentleman who cheerfully waves his hand at the board on the wall, asking, "What movie would you like to see tonight?"

The board is lit up with dramas, documentaries, thrillers, action movies, romances and more. Every genre that you could think of is on the board, but the movie title remains the same: *Life Re-Scripted*. Each genre could take you down a different path for the next few hours, or

24

in the case of your life on the big screen, for the next few years (if not more).

You see, you've been on this path that has been set forth and paved by those before you and the great sages that have lived even before them. Your parents or role models have altered the path, and should you be lacking either parents or role models, the path still shifts, because you are alive and making choices. Remember this: the path will constantly change, but it is up to you to determine where it leads. No more blaming anyone else. You are in the driver's seat now.

When I think about the path that I've been on in my twenty-six years on this earth, I remember back to the time I was first learning how to write with a pencil. I know this sounds quite odd, but you'll understand why this makes perfect sense in just a moment.

When I was growing up, my mom was an occupational therapist who worked with special needs children. She would assist them in learning the simple acts of living, like how to read and write, or even how to eat their food properly. Every now and then, I got the opportunity to go to work with her and "play."

But there is a very particular day I will never forget when she came home and wanted to use me as her test subject for a new tool she received. It was an oddly shaped piece of foam which wrapped around your pencil or pen and was ergonomically fitted to teach you how to hold the pencil properly. Mom handed it to me and showed me how to hold it. I'm sure my face more than likely told her what I thought of this thing without words even being necessary.

Being the rebel that I was, as a child, I always got some weird satisfaction in disappointing my elders or revolting against instruction. So when it came time for my mom to teach me how to properly hold a pencil, she covered up my writing utensil with this odd foam thing that made the pencil thicker and harder to hold than I could on my own. I pretended to do my work until the teacher walked away and then I had immediately reverted back to my own ways.

It was awkward and it was painful, but I taught myself how to improperly hold a pencil for the sheer satisfaction of not doing what I was instructed to do. I'm sure you can relate. Later on in college, I was fortunate enough that laptops were nearly a requirement, so I never had to write a paper by hand again. And as a film major, I never really had written exams, just video projects.

I tell you this story to acknowledge that life is going to throw a bunch of "supposed tos" at you, and a lot of the time, you won't want to follow the script to a T. You'll pitch fits, you'll whine, you'll kick and stomp your feet, and you'll resist the urge to follow the norm. When the teacher is watching, you might stick to the plan, but the second she walks out of the classroom, you know what happens.

Let me ask you this…

Have you ever felt like there was a path that you were being forced into? Perhaps you grew up thinking you absolutely had to become a doctor or a lawyer because that was what your parents were pushing you to do. Better yet, maybe you come from a long line of accountants or farmers, and you felt like it was your job to carry on the family name and reputation.

I felt like this when I was growing up. I thought that my life was supposed to be played out in a certain way. Here's a script that might sound familiar to you:

I'm supposed to go to school to get good grades and get into college.

I'm supposed to go to college to get a degree so I can find a good job.

I'm supposed to get a job to pay off the debt of going to college.

I'm supposed to pay off my debt to afford a family and hopefully live a comfortable life.

I'm supposed to live a comfortable life to ultimately save up for a retirement.

I'm supposed to save up for a retirement to afford retirement and leave something behind when I die.

And if I'm lucky, and if I do it right, I'll have enough money to sell my house, move to Florida, join all the slow-driving seniors, and play cards with the boys while we drink stale coffee and complain about how cold it is because our taste buds have been burnt off from the past seventy-five years of abuse at the local drive-through or coffee franchise.

I don't know about you, but this sounds awful. This sounds like a life not lived to the fullest. When I think of this "standard" or "script" that has been prescribed for us to follow, the little kindergartner in me starts kicking and screaming and chucking his stupid ergonomic pencil across the room screaming for a grilled cheese and a TV show in his blanket fort.

I started to ask around and talk to my friends about why I felt this way, and I found that I wasn't the only quarter-lifer, as my friend Adam 'Smiley' Poswolsky would call it, who thought this set of guidelines was nonsense.

In *The Quarter-Life Breakthrough*, it was Adam who said, "It's okay to want something different than you did two years ago. It's okay to leave a job everyone else thinks is awesome, and it's okay not to know exactly what it is you want..." And at one point in 2014, I found myself sitting with him in a coffee shop in San Francisco, trying to figure out where I should go next. Despite being called lazy or unmotivated, we settle for the script and give up chasing after a meaningful life.

But why would we live our lives like this, working purposeful jobs to pay bills for things we're not even sure we want, if there were so many other seemingly better options out there?

So back to this whole choosing a path and figuring out what genre of a movie you'd like to see. Your life is a fishbowl of decisions and risks. Some choices you make will have more negative consequences, while many will have none at all. You'll have times of romance and you'll have times of horror. There will be moments of drama contrasted with moments of adventure or introspection.

If we're lucky, the scarier moments will come with warning music much like the ominous JAWS movie sound effects and if you are really lucky, you won't have a mouth full of nachos and malted milk balls when the hilarious parts occur.

But if there is one thing that is true: all of these genres will be available to you, and in many cases, you get to decide which path to go down.

A Re-Script in My Life

In May of 2013, I was working a full-time job at one of the Genius Bars at an Apple Store. I saw people day in and day out who had chosen every possible path, from doctors and lawyers to photographers and ex-convicts. I saw disability and I saw ability. Looking back on it all now, it was a very rewarding experience because I learned to work with people. But at the time, I couldn't really see the value in the experience. It's funny how you can only connect the dots looking back (Thanks, Steve Jobs, for teaching me that one).

I'll never forget the day I chose to change the genre of my story from a stagnant drama to one of action and adventure. As the band Jack's Mannequin would say, "And today was a day just like any other." I went into work and donned my infamous blue t-shirt with a white fruit logo dead center of the chest. I wore my black rimmed plastic glasses that were a signature to many of the employees there, grabbed my iPad to see my schedule for the day, and walked out onto the floor. It was numb routine, the wash, rinse, repeat cycle of a corporate 9-5er.

It was a Sunday. I remember this because Sundays were typically our busiest days and that's when all the crazies liked to come out after church. Hundreds of people flocked through the store, looking to make purchases, asking to have their phones fixed, and wanting to learn how to edit vacation photos.

I was standing about three quarters of the way back into the store and my particular role that day was to play gatekeeper. I checked people in for their tech appointments, made notes as to what they needed help with, and assisted anyone without an appointment in signing up for one. You could call me the air traffic controller, in a sense. I was keeping an eye on the queue to speed up or slow down the work based on the demand and our ability to keep up as a team.

I looked up after assisting someone to their seat, just as this woman came stomping through the front door. She asked our greeter whom she needed to talk with about a broken phone. He hesitantly pointed in my direction, because she had 'I don't have an appointment but you need to fix this now or I'm going Hiroshima on your ass' written all over her forehead. She locked eyes on me. Right then and there, I knew I was going to quit my job.

It was people like this person that made me feel hopeless for humanity because the verbal abuse I was about to endure was proportional to an all out war.

The customer came stomping to the back of the room. Her feet were positively booming against the Italian stone floor. My first thought was, *Uh oh.*

The front door person had just enough time to radio back to me on the headset that she had dropped her phone in the toilet and she was livid—as if I couldn't tell from her body language. She chucked the iPhone into my hand and started yelling immediately how it was my fault that her phone wound up in the toilet, that it was freezing up as it was and she hated that stupid thing and all of the sudden the world was coming to an end because she had a tiny accident.

Now I'm normally a very sympathetic person, but I knew that this encounter was just like any other. I asked if she had an appointment, waited for her bewildered response because she had no idea she needed one. And as the backlash ensued, I started to tune out her voice. She went full kindergartner mode. I had seen this before, but it had been about two decades since I witnessed this type of behavior this close in front of me.

While I tuned out the shouting and jumped on the rocket ship to my happy place so I could keep a smile on my face, I noticed someone in the corner of the store who was watching. One of my former freelance videography clients was standing there, checking out an iPad, but he was distracted by the scene that was unfolding. My heart sank when I caught his gaze, because a wealthy business owner whom I looked up to as a role model was witnessing this embarrassing event.

After our plain-clothes security officers in the store removed the disturbance, this man walked over to me and asked what I was doing for dinner that night. Little did I know that this night would shift the genre of my story for the rest of my life. This very moment was the beginning of my life being re-scripted.

The workday passed and eventually I walked down to the steakhouse at the other end of the mall where he was meeting me for dinner. I ran down the hall while changing out of my blue shirt because I didn't want to be late. We got seated and he asked me, "What are you doing here?" to which I replied, "I'm not really sure. You asked me to dinner!" Ever the smartass I was...

He proceeded to ask why I was still working for someone else and asked about the far too common occurrences of angry customers abusing my ego for hours on end. Ultimately, he stopped the conversation on a dime and asked the waitress for a bar napkin. He pulled out a fancy pen inscribed with his initials from his suit jacket. I didn't even think I would ever afford a jacket that nice. I didn't even know how I was going to pay for dinner that night.

He asked how much money I was making. It was an hourly job, but essentially my salary estimate was about $30,000 a year. This was surely no sign of success or advancement in life, but it was what it was. He asked me if I knew how to make $30,000 in a year, and the only answer I could think of was work at the Apple Store or find another job that would suffice. Job... I despise that word now looking back because it implies that I have to live by guidelines that are being written by someone else. But I digress.

He instructed me to open the calculator on my phone and to do some math. If I worked only five days out of the week for fifty weeks out of the year (leaving me one sick week and one vacation week), I would be working two hundred and fifty days a year. He first instructed me however to calculate 30,000 divided by twelve, which comes out to 2,500 per month.

When I broke down the math even further, it came out to one hundred and twenty dollars a day working two hundred and fifty days a year. Now at the time, I lived in a neighborhood of nearly one hundred houses, and if I cut the lawns or plowed the snow for five of those neighbors, I could make one hundred and twenty dollars in a single day.

Things started to click after he pointed this out. It wasn't that I was guaranteed to land every neighbor of mine as a client and even more important, I wasn't going to start a lawn mowing or driveway shoveling business, so the task itself was irrelevant. The important factor in this conversation was that he had proven to me that I no longer had this gloomy goal of making a $30,000 income, but rather the goal of $120 per day for five days out of the week.

He then proceeded to ask me how I could make $60,000 in one year. The answer was just as simple. Do double the work or double your prices.

After talking through a few more ideas, we both came to the agreement that my freelance skill of videography was worthy of a full-time pursuit. I was a bit worried because I had never done work on a professional level before, but everyone needs to start somewhere.

Needless to say, I walked into my job the next day and put in my resignation letter and two weeks notice. I nearly gave my Jewish mother a heart attack when I told her, but my mind had been made up and I was beyond the point of no return. The genre was changing, the script was being re-written and I was now taking a fork in the road that hadn't previously revealed itself to me.

Every movie theater that you walk into is going to have a different number of screens, different show times and even different movies. You might find that some of the titles are the same across location but some theaters may have action and adventure films while others play the indie documentary films and the romances depending on the week. The genres are different but a story is always being told.

Throughout your life, you will encounter twists and turns that will allow you to choose a different story. Think of it like those books we read as kids where it told you to turn to page 86 if you want the main character to fight off the evil dragon, or turn to page 42 if you want him to run away. There's always another option, a way out. Sometimes it takes a different line of thinking to figure it out, but I believe that you have full control over your story genre.

It's time for you to choose a movie, to start an experience with a certain genre. It's time for you to buy your ticket—your ticket to a life re-scripted.

Life Re-Scripted Action Steps

- Take a deep breath and understand that life gets started when you get started.

- Have a pep talk with yourself about the changes that are about to occur in your life. Remind yourself that this is going to be exciting, confusing and at times frustrating all at once but it will pay off in the end.

- Write a promise to yourself that you wish to uphold over the next twelve months and tape it to the fridge or mirror so that you see it every day.

- Find comfort in a friend or a family member that will support you regardless of your life choices.

- Remember that your path will constantly change without giving notice. Identify the moment where you were fed up with a mediocre life and harness that energy to take the next leap.

- Choose your own destiny and turn to the next page.

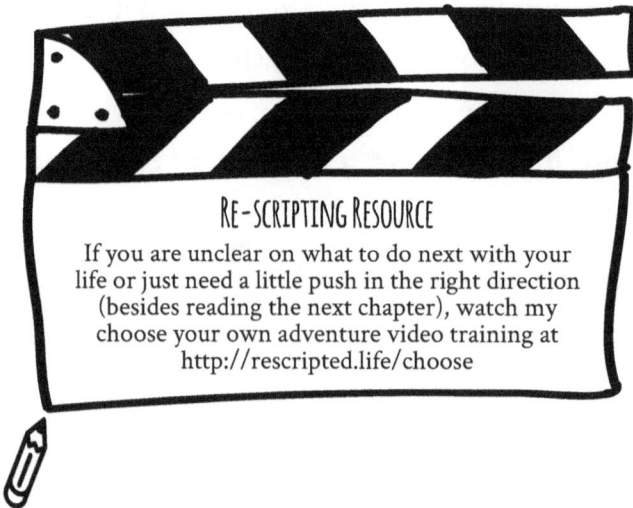

Re-Scripting Resource

If you are unclear on what to do next with your life or just need a little push in the right direction (besides reading the next chapter), watch my choose your own adventure video training at http://rescripted.life/choose

Concessions are Available in the Lobby

"You are educated. Your certification is in your degree. You may think of it as the ticket to the good life. Let me ask you to think of an alternative. Think of it as your ticket to change the world."

–Tom Brokaw

In chapter two, I'm going to share with you the three P's of viewing your story. These are the enhancements so to speak. Think of them like the candy counter at the movie theater—everything is there as an add-on to your movie-watching experience. I'm going to share with you my Always Be Moving Principle which ensures that you have a prosperous and ever-changing life.

The funny thing about most of these principles is you might learn them and think, *Well duh*, and that's OK, because the real methods for finding purpose, becoming successful and living a life you are passionate about are right in front of you. Just like in a movie theater they are being handed to us on a silver platter, we just have to pay the asking price.

The definition of insanity is doing the same thing over and over again and expecting different results. If you don't implement the changes you want to see in your life, then you will get the same results you've always had. You're not insane, but this could sure drive you insane if you don't see the change. After making the change, it all comes down to the follow up. Be sure to go back and reexamine what you did, make tweaks to it, and keep doing it. And make sure not to give up when it doesn't quite work out the way you wanted.

🎬

Ticket in hand, you walk through the glass doors, and typically you'd be greeted by someone collecting tickets and directing you to the theater for your showing. It's time to grab one more thing, though, before you run into the theater. The warm smell of popcorn is stronger than ever, and the glass cases filled with every candy imaginable are calling your name.

Watching a movie at the theater isn't the same as lying in bed with Netflix. It's an experience that requires you to actively be a part of it rather than make a few button clicks. While sometimes it's nice to enjoy the show passively, there is a different type of excitement that comes from going out to see a performance. The question is, are you really going to lie there and watch in bed every Friday night? Or are you going to get out and really experience the whole thing?

At the concession stand you have even more options, as if choosing the genre of your film wasn't hard enough. You could go for the nachos and grab a large soda to wash the salt off your lips. Better yet, the Super Freezee machine has a red light on showing that it's cooled and ready.

Despite it being a $12 beverage, you spring for the blue raspberry Super Freezee and pay the extra fifty cents to get the largest size they offer. Just in case you weren't satisfied by that, you throw in a box of chocolate covered cookie dough and a small popcorn to round off this combo.

What I'm getting at here is that there are tons of options when it comes to enhancements for your viewing pleasure. And there's a delicate balance at play because you don't want to go all dairy or you know your stomach will kick you out of the theater just when the movie is getting to the good part. And if you get a large soda, you'll have to pee more than once throughout the movie.

As a teenager, I used to go with my friends Jason and Jake to the movies on the weekend. They were twins, so this always made for good entertainment, seeing as they were at each other's throats before their mom even got us to the theater. And being the rebels that we were, instead of going into the theater and buying the overpriced concessions, we'd get their mom to drop us off at the mall next door and buy all our candy and cheeseburgers in the food court. We'd stuff it in our cargo shorts and sneak into movie after movie.

I've always been in love with the theaters since I was a kid. There's something about being fully immersed in the experience. If you are a true rebel, you'll discover your own concessions to sneak in with you through life that will enhance your experience. But for now, I'm going to make it really easy for you.

I've found three concessions, or enhancements, if you will, that must be balanced in the story of your life to ensure maximum viewing pleasure.

- Patience
- Passion
- Perseverance

PATIENCE

Patience is something that most people are either too good at or are lacking. For example, after I left my full time job in May of 2013, I was disappointed that I didn't have any clients come in for the first few weeks. The movie *Field of Dreams* says, "If you build it, he will come," but that just isn't true. I built a business; I got business cards and an accountant; I did everything that I thought I was supposed to do; and yet, I had nothing to show for it. There I went again, trying to follow the script.

Don't forget that the millionaires of Facebook and the Silicon Valley were not made millionaires overnight. In fact, most of these entrepreneurs worked for months, years and sometimes even decades to get to where they are now. A big key in patience is losing your sense of entitlement and coming back to humility. Stay humble and realize that you have chosen a journey (entrepreneurship or not) that takes blood, sweat and tears to turn into a reality. If it was easy, everyone would be doing it right?

Patience can be a curse, too, and here is what I mean by that. Having too much patience, or feeling content, can lead to mediocrity and stagnation. I have watched friends stay in relationships and in jobs that they don't like for years longer than they should have, because it was easier than ending it. Why would you choose to suffer though when the grass is greener on the other side and you can look out the window to see proof of that?

Being patient for too long and thinking that the world is just going to pan out exactly how you expected is a mistake and a hard lesson for many. I think back to the quote, "Nothing moves until you do." I don't remember who said it first, and perhaps I made it up, off of some other quote. But the truth is in that one word: move. Hospital patients often end up with bigger issues than what they went in for because they lie in a bed all day. Muscle degeneration, circulation issues, you name it. The key to living a long and prosperous life is the ABM Principle. Always Be Moving.

I remember ABM when I think of patience, because if our stoicism isn't allowing us to advance in life, then we need to take a look around at why we aren't moving forward. Patience is useful if you are waiting in line for a ticket at the theater, because eventually you will get to the front. You know this because you've been there on a Friday night when the place is jam-packed.

Patience is not going to be useful to you, however, if you are sitting in a theater and the kid behind you keeps purposefully kicking your chair to get a rise out of you. This is why I say to use caution when you are being patient, and remember that balance is key.

Passion

Passion is an amazing driver for advancement. When I first discovered my passion for storytelling, everything started to fall into place from that moment on. I was sitting in a mastermind group made up of myself and two other business owners. I was sharing my frustration with my video production company, and as the words were coming out of my mouth, one of the others turned to me and hurriedly asked me to repeat what I had just said.

I discovered that videography itself was not necessarily the thing I was passionate about. Rather it was the people sharing their stories in a way that could evoke emotions in others. People won't remember what you did, but they'll remember how you made them feel.

There is no coincidence that this occurred right around the same time as I started my podcast, *The Year of Purpose Podcast*. On this show, I interviewed over one-hundred people from all over the globe who built a life on their own terms so that I could share the possibilities with others. If you are interested in tuning in to the podcast, head on over to http://www.yearofpurpose.com where you can listen to all of our episodes for free. I very quickly became passionate about every piece of the puzzle in making the podcast a success. While the podcast didn't produce an income for me for the first nine months, that wasn't a concern of mine. I knew that if I kept working on it, and as long as my passion was still in it 100%, I would find success and make a difference in the lives of others.

Passion is a double-edged sword, just as patience is. If I were to become so passionate about my podcast that I dropped my full-time income producing activities entirely, I would quickly find it tough to pay the rent. Passion has to be tamed at certain points and brought back down to a reasonable level so that it doesn't override our basic instincts of reality and logic.

PERSEVERANCE

Last but not least is perseverance. I really see this as the secret bonus ingredient to the mix. Patience is kind of like the Super Freezee at the theater: if you drink it too fast, you'll get brain freeze; if you drink it too slowly, the ice melts and all you are left with is watered-down syrup. Neither one makes for a pleasurable movie-going experience. Passion is much like the butter on the popcorn—too much passion and you lose the popcorn to a mouthful of salty liquid and hands covered in grease; not enough butter and you don't even want to eat the popcorn anymore because it simply has no flavor.

Perseverance is the bag of gummy worms or the box of chocolate drops that you open up part of the way into the movie. You take little bites at a time because you want it to last. You could shovel down the whole box at once, but then you'll have nothing left and be disappointed and you aren't even a third of the way through the previews. Perseverance is for the long haul. You need little doses of it throughout life, because every new obstacle that presents itself could be the point where you give up.

At just thirteen years old, I remember going back to school after Thanksgiving like any other day. In my English class, they made this announcement over the intercom stating that they were very sorry that we had lost a fellow student and that guidance counselors would be available to us if we needed someone to talk to.

At first I had no idea who it was, but as it is in middle school, word can travel really fast. I soon found out that it was a boy who had been in tons of my classes. I had seen him plenty of times before and I had known him. I had talked to him. I wouldn't have considered him a friend but definitely an acquaintance. I learned that on Thanksgiving day, he had ventured into the office of his father, who was a police officer, and he took his father's gun out of the desk drawer and decided to take his own life.

A lot of questions ran through my mind at this point. While some people were breaking down into tears, I sat there silently and took it all in. Even in times of sadness or struggle, I can't even start to stress how important is just to take it all in and be there in the moment to feel... anything.

Around this time, I remember my parents taking me to go see a therapist. I think I refused to talk to the first one. It took about five or six psychiatrists before I actually found one that I was even willing to open up to or to talk with. My memory from this time in my life was a bit hazy. Not only was I dealing with the feelings of depression and suicide, around that time but I also found out that I had what they called a panic and anxiety disorder.

So I'd have moments throughout the day, sometimes thirty, forty, or fifty, where I would have to lie down in bed, sit in a corner, or lock myself in a room curled in a fetal position. I would take my fingers and stick them in my ears and try to block out all sound or noise because I just couldn't cope.

It made me feel like I was going to throw up out of the sheer fact that I could see or hear or experience things going on outside of my own body. If you have never had them, panic attacks are quite possibly the worst experience in the world. It's worse than pain, because you honestly just feel like you're going to die, and it does get to point where you almost become OK with that happening. I know I sure did.

The problem was that I didn't die. At least, I thought at the time that it was a problem, because I wanted to live, but I was stuck in this emotion and this feeling and I couldn't even shake it and I couldn't die so I couldn't get out of it. That's a really tough place to be, because at that point you're almost ready to take your own life because you want to stop all this craziness.

Now, some people experience these attacks once a day, sometimes only once a week or once a month. I was getting them every ten or twenty minutes. It was an absolute nightmare. They wouldn't go away. I didn't understand them and how I could control them, and my parents just sent me to a doctor.

After being placed on a cocktail of medications, I was numb to everything, but I was still able to feel anger and I was still able to feel sadness. Those were probably the only two emotions that weren't numbed out for me. But this isn't about how I got to my lowest, deepest, darkest point of depression. This is about how I overcame it and it's absolutely crazy looking back on this, because in my eyes I have no idea how it happened. You can call it a miracle. You can call it what you will, but I'll never forget that one day.

I woke up and walked into the kitchen and I took a look at my medicine bottles lined up on the counter. I decided that I was just going to go sit down in the living room for a moment. So I walked past the pills and sat down on the couch. I can picture myself sitting there, feet up on the couch and hugging my legs in tight. I sat there rocking back and forth, and I can't even imagine all the thoughts that went through my head, but I remember telling myself, "I can't do this anymore."

Perseverance was kicking in. The voice in my head that said I can't do this anymore was speaking up.

I felt that was the morning where I had officially given in. I had given up. I was okay if my heart had just stopped. I was okay if my lungs stopped functioning. I was okay if I took a knife to my wrist and sliced it all the way down. I was okay taking a bottle of medicine out of the cabinet and just swallowing as many as I possibly could.

I had accepted my fate. And, in a sense, I had already died. Patience and passion were gone. I think what I learned from this is that in order to come back from a moment like that, you almost have to die, or at least the part of you that wants to leave the earth needs to die.

You almost have to be willing to lose everything because when you're at a point when you have nothing left to lose, there's only one way to go. You've got everything to gain.

I sat there staring out into our back yard, telling myself, "I can't do this anymore. I can't do this anymore." It played over and over in my head until I had this small moment of clarity where I turned it around and I said, "What can I do?"

I don't know what came over me right then, but I had this moment in which I was able to step outside of my own body, out of my own mind, and out of my own emotions, and say to myself, "If I have nothing left to do on this earth, what could I do?" The option came to me. I realized that I could live. I had a choice, but it would be only what I made of it.

I didn't necessarily see it as a probable option at the time, but I had been able to see it as an option nonetheless. I did something that I would never advise anyone else to do. I sat there and I said, "I'm not going to take my medicine today and tomorrow I'm going to wake up and I'm going to try to just get up out of bed."

I went to the medicine on the counter. I counted the pills out and made it look like I'd taken them. At that point, my mom wasn't policing me anymore, because I had been on it all for so long, but she was still refilling the bottles so I had to make it look like they were going away. It was easy—I would just take the pills and flush them down the toilet. I didn't tell anyone.

The first day I didn't really notice anything because withdrawal didn't really kick in for a solid twenty-four hours. So what I did is go to bed. I just lay there in bed for the rest of the day, and I felt the same emotions I'd felt for the past few months. I let it go, and then ultimately the sun went down, and I went to sleep. I woke up the next morning and my head started to feel slightly clearer.

I woke up extremely upset. I woke up still wanting to harm myself, actually now more than ever, but I felt lucid. It was like having a sinus infection for a week, then suddenly waking up and it was all cleared up.

I went back to the questions. "I woke up. Now, what if I could do more?" It was the perseverance once again, winning.

I wouldn't call myself cured, because the worst was yet to come. I was angry. I was furious. I wanted to break things. I wanted to put my arm through a wall. I remember actually standing there and punching a wall a couple of times and feeling pain for the first time in a very long time. I hadn't really felt pain for a year or two. My medicine, especially the tranquilizer, had me so numb to it. But now, I started to feel things.

This went on for about a week. It went to everything from pulling a knife out of the kitchen drawer to pulling bottles of pills out of the closet to sitting there and thinking "Well, I could just drown myself in the bathtub right now." And for some reason, at the end of every day, I would stand up. I would put the knife and the pills away, and I would go to bed.

I think that it was the lesson that I learned from my classmate. He made the choice to take his own life. That meant that I had options, too, and it was up to me. But there were so many more reasons why I could live. It was just a bit tougher to realize in the middle of all that.

Now at this time it was very hard to see a future for myself. I didn't really have any aspirations, but I saw a choice. In that moment when you feel stuck or as if this is the end, when you've pretty much accepted your fate, what is so important is to realize is that there is always a choice, and that it's completely up to you to choose. And when that choice arises, you have to give yourself every reason in the world to follow the choice that your heart desires. Persevere. At the gut, self-preserving level, your heart's desire, your hard wiring, is to live.

I wasn't sure when I started writing whether or not I'd share my battles with depression, anxiety and suicide, but I've learned it's more common than I thought. I share this not for sympathy or for someone to look at me and think, *Oh, he's had a tough life.* My story is important because I learned how to change my situation even while under the toughest of scenarios. This is to prove by example that no matter how hopeless you might feel, and despite the turmoil, you, too, can make it back to a safe place and start over.

The three P's can save your life when balanced properly. I'm not saying a Super Freezee and a box of popcorn are going to save your life at the movies. In fact, if you eat them often enough, you would be risking heart attack. It's a matter of having all three work in unison. Much like how you can't go and get just the nachos at the concession stand; you'll need a soda to go with it because the chips are really salty.

But they sure will enhance your experience for the time being, brain freeze and all.

LIFE RE-SCRIPTED ACTION STEPS

- Crush the cycle of insanity and jump off the hamster wheel. The wash, rinse, repeat cycle no longer serves you so change up your morning routine and throw a curve ball in from time to time.

- Develop patience by learning how to cook. We often forget how much effort goes into preparing our food. Start cooking and planning your meals for the week on the weekend for a healthier diet and a lesson in waiting for the reward.

- Grow your passions in life by jumping into new social circles and picking up new activities. Leverage sites like Meetup.com to find fun new groups.

- Build your confidence and your ability to persevere by writing a self-talk mantra. Create a saying like "Don't forget to breathe" or, "Take every risk, drop every fear" that you can repeat to yourself in times of stress.

RE-SCRIPTING RESOURCE

If you want to learn how to create your own mantra so that you can break through the next obstacle that comes your way, watch my video training on how to design a mantra at http://rescripted.life/mantra

Take Your Seat

"Movies touch our hearts, and awaken our vision, and change the way we see things. They take us to other places. They open doors and minds. Movies are the memories of our lifetime. We need to keep them alive."

–Martin Scorsese

Now it's time to pick a spot for your movie. It's important to note that there are good seats and there are bad seats when it comes to watching the story of your life. Pick a good one and it will combine with the three P's to make an excellent life experience. But pick a bad one, and you may end up getting the kid that kicks your seat for ninety minutes straight.

We're going to talk about gratitude in just a moment and how it is one of the greatest gifts we have been offered in life. But first we're going to talk about how you show up in the world and what you want your role to be like in life. I'll share the limiting perspective that our loved ones and friends might take that could prevent us from reaching our fullest potential, and how your reactions to events in life are a direct indicator of how your story will play out.

One of the best parts about getting to the movie early is that you have your choice of seats. Often times, the ideal seat isn't exactly front and center. In most theaters, the seats directly in front are so close to the screen that you have to strain your neck to look up just to see what is going on the entire movie. This reminds me of how it's possible to lose yourself in your life: when you're so far into the situation that you can't take a step back to see the whole picture.

When you're at the movies, you want the best seat in the house. You want the seat where the sound is even on both sides, so it doesn't sound like a fire truck is coming from behind you when it's really right in front of you on the screen. You want to be as close to the center of the screen as possible so you don't have your neck turned for the entire movie. And it's helpful to have a comfy seat for the ride.

There are many other factors that make for having a good experience, like making sure the floor beneath your seat isn't sticky, avoiding sitting behind the tall people or making sure that you don't sit in front of someone who talks the whole movie while kicking your chair.

So how do you choose the best seat in the house when it comes to life? What should you be looking out for or trying to avoid?

It all starts with showing up with the intention of getting the best seat. How do you want to show up to the world? Do you want to be the take-action person who holds responsibility for your decisions and your life? Or do you want to be the person who always has that "Woe is me," victim mentality and wants to blame other people for what's going wrong in your life?

I get it that it's much easier to blame someone else for your problems because it relieves you of the responsibility of life. You no longer have to take action to make a difference. You can just accept that this is your truth and your reality. But this doesn't fix the underlying issue – the issue is you.

It's harsh, I know, but we've become a culture of bandaiders. I know that isn't even a word but I'm calling us bandaiders because we are very good at covering up festering wounds. We don't see the negative sides of life because no one wants to deal with it. No one knows how to deal with their own lives, and nobody wants to deal with someone else's mess.

So let me ask you this again, how are you showing up to the world? Are you showing up on time with your freshly buttered popcorn and ready for the action? Or are you running in at the last minute, grabbing a seat in the front row because that's all that is left and missing out on the best possible experience?

Adam 'Smiley' Poswolsky, author of *The Quarter-Life Breakthrough*, said, "Why would you be doing anything less than reaching your full potential in life? But I hadn't really asked myself that and once I did, I just sat there like 'Why the hell would I be doing anything else than reaching my full potential in life?' And that was kind of the moment where I knew I had to make the leap...and I had to quit my job. That was kind of when it all just clicked...understanding that by not leaving... I was actually robbing others of the difference I could be making because I wasn't really unleashing my full potential on the world... When you realize that actually it's quite powerful."

Smiley got it. It took creating this powerful moment for himself where he sat down and really questioned what type of a seat he wanted to take in his life.

The Blocked View

There's nothing worse than grabbing a seat and someone comes and sits down directly in front of you to block your view. It's a pain, but they probably didn't even realize they were doing it. Throughout life, even before you get to the hard parts, you are going to have people, situations, circumstances and objects that are going to plop themselves down right in front of you, distorting your view.

I remember when I walked into that Apple Store and told my coworker, John, that I was going to quit. John was a great guy. He had been there for a few years and was extremely passionate about photography, so we always had things in common to talk about. But when I told him I was going to quit, he responded with, "You won't do it." I can still hear it in his voice, "You won't do it."

Don't get me wrong. John is a neat guy and I wish him all the best in the world, but hearing someone tell you that you can't or that you won't was extremely discouraging. He was an obstacle in the way of me seeing the bigger picture. Not a bad person, but a bad message. His message was limited to his own beliefs. The funny thing is, about three years later, I looked him up and he was starting to take the steps in his own life to become happier. He was looking for a way out, the exact thing that I had just discovered a few years prior.

It's funny how things work out when you set the example.

Have you ever been talking to someone and heard the words, "I could never do that," or, "That will never work." And you instantly deflate and think that your idea might not be as good as you thought? Of course you have! We constantly do this both to ourselves and to others! This is the obstacle that we never asked for, that we never placed in front of ourselves, yet now it has walked up and sat down directly in front of us.

If you are getting to the movies too early, you'll be the first one in the theater and it's much harder to avoid having that person sit in front of you. If you get in while everyone else is filing in, you'll still have time to pick a good spot or even move to a different one. Timing is everything, and being aware of your surroundings can help ensure that those who might otherwise block your vision for your life can be avoided.

The Sticky Floor

So what do you do if you've avoided the tall guy, you've successfully landed a seat that isn't in the front row and you are just about to sit down, but you realize the floor is sticky? Almost every aspect about your situation is just perfect, but there's one little thing making you feel uncomfortable about it all. What do you do?

I think back to the story of Adam Hommey, an amazingly talented website expert that I interviewed on my podcast. Here's a piece of his story about how sometimes things just don't work out the way you wanted, but ultimately, as my favorite college professor always said, "I take chicken shit and I turn it into chicken salad."

Adam shares his experience with smashing a printer *Office Space*-style, and how it led him to a great revelation:

"So here I am, that morning—as I said, I ran out of food. Even though I had money for food, I'd run out of food and I'd eaten toothpaste for breakfast that morning. And after dealing with the latest crisis of existential proportions, I needed to print something out of my printer that my accountant desperately needed me to sign and fax back to him so he could file something…So between one disaster and another, I hit print on my computer to print out a piece of paper.

"In the middle of printing out the page, the printer decides to cancel the job on me because it says it ran out of ink. And I'm thinking, *You could not have told me half a page ago that you ran out of ink? You could not have warned me that it was running low on ink? You could not have wasted this piece of paper that I don't have time to replace because you couldn't tell me you ran out of ink?*

"Next thing you know, [mimics smashing the printer].

"A year and a half later, when I moved out of that apartment, I was still finding pieces of that printer. I didn't drop it on the floor just once, I up and dropped it several times… So here I am. I'm at a very low place right now. I'm thinking, *I just smashed my printer because it ran out of ink.*

"I thought to myself, *You know, I'm having a really bad day here. I'm not enjoying my business very much and something just happened here that caused me to go over the edge. But I can draw a line right now and say that right now, up until this moment, I have allowed frustration, overwhelm, and lack of testicular fortitude to get in the way of my success. From this point forward, I claim a successful business with balance and proper management of time…* and whatever else was coming in my head at the moment."

There's a favorite saying of mine and I hear it playing in my head quite often when I'm in the middle of something that is uncomfortable. The saying is, "Embrace the suck," and that's just what Adam did there. While your situation right now might not be ideal, you can still make the most out of it. We might be able to avoid a lot of nasty situations or just barely scrape past what could have been a bad scenario, but life won't be perfect. There's no magic wand that is going to make every situation perfect.

So is the sticky floor going to ruin the whole show for you?

Gratitude — the Best Seat in the House

At this exact point in time right now, for you, living a purposeful life may seem as though it's not an option. The door hasn't been opened to you yet, and you don't know all the secrets to living happily each and every day. Thousands of so-called "gurus" and "experts" will tell you that they know the secret to life and how you can be happy all the time, but that's simply not true.

There is a way, however, for you to feel gratitude all the time, and in a moment, I'm going to share with you how a small change can ripple outward and affect every aspect of your life.

My friend Corey Jahnke said to me, "So people tell me often what a horrible place the world is. But there's other people who tell me what a beautiful place the world is. There's other people that tell me "Well, the world's just an okay place." Here's the reality: The world is, was, and has always been an awful place, an okay place, or a wonderful place, depending on what you go looking for. So when you surround yourself with negative people, and all you do is watch negative news and search out negative stories on the Internet, your world is negative. But when you become a positive, amazing person surrounding yourself with positive, like attracts like."

So when it comes to opening up that door and opening your mind to the possibilities, it has to start from a place of gratitude and positivity.

Gratitude is something that we talk about quite often, but it seems we're never very good at practicing it. I believe that gratitude is the one thing that was not quite open to my brain before starting my personal development journey. Now, gratitude is in my bag of tricks when it comes to getting unstuck from my life, when I am trying to embrace the suck and find the silver lining. I'm willing to bet it's something you could benefit from more of as well.

In his TED Talk titled *The Happy Secret to Better Work*, Shawn Achor proposed a strategy that could radically change your views on life each and every day. He researched and experimented, and ultimately determined that twenty-one days was all it took to alter your state of mind.

So I took the challenge and actually extended it to thirty days just to make sure it would really stick. I like habits that stick because this means I don't have to go through the sucky part of retraining myself over and over to remember them.

Here's what he recommended you do to create lasting positive change in your life. Be sure to do these each and every day:

- Write down three gratitudes—three things you're thankful for
- Journal for ten minutes
- Exercise
- Meditate
- Complete at least one random act of kindness

I challenged myself to a full month of doing this, and now, even in the darkest of situations, I find myself capable of finding a silver lining. I know it sounds crazy, but I guarantee you if you open up your mind to the possibility that this could change your life, you will see a difference.

Think about this for a moment. The very fact that you can afford a fifteen-dollar movie (because let's be real, they're expensive), the fact that you had change left over for snacks (that you didn't have to buy), and the fact that you had the time to take off from your busy schedule to escape from the world for a little bit… isn't that something you should be grateful for?

But the truth is, we should be grateful that when we're sick we can lie in bed and still be entertained. We should be grateful that every night when we go to sleep there's either air conditioning or a fan to keep us from getting too warm. We should be grateful.

Remember back when I told you all of those "supposed tos" that really didn't support you living your best life? If there is any one "supposed to" that should be followed, it would be that you are supposed to practice gratitude.

There's a poster in my office that says, "Every day may not be good but there is something good in every day." One of the best parts about being in sticky situations is that you can unstick them.

I firmly believe that there is always a way out. You might not like the fact that you'll have to scrape the gum off of your shoe after leaving the theater, but once you do, the stickiness goes away, right? Find the small silver lining and really express gratitude for it verbally, mentally, on paper, however you so choose. But do it.

The Obnoxious Moviegoers

Last, but certainly not least, is how will you react to others? If you're sitting in the theater and someone just won't shut up, are you going to be the one who stands up and yells at them in front of a sold-out crowd? Are you going to sit there and try your best to tune them out? Are you going to ruin your friend's time by talking to her about how obnoxious the other moviegoers are?

Your reactions are a direct reflection of you. Only you have control over how you react, despite the fact that it may seem you are simply reacting to a certain event. You still have the choice to speak up, sit down or shut up. Stop making excuses for why you react in a certain way to the events in your life. You were given the opportunity to show up and pick out the best seat in the house and make the most out of it. The question is, will you show up during the previews or have you missed the opening credits entirely?

The only way to find out is by silencing your cell phones and getting ready to sit back to enjoy the show.

Life Re-Scripted Action Steps

- Avoid the *woe is me* mentality by remembering that like will attract like, negativity will only attract negativity. Snap out of feeling bad for yourself and remember that you have the courage to take a new path.

🎬 Approach tensions head on without resorting to the first aid kit for bandages. If something comes up in your life, take care of it immediately instead of sweeping it under the rug.

🎬 Buy yourself a notebook and keep a journal. Notebooks can help when you have ideas that are clouding your vision for the day. Write down the blips on your radar to keep them for later and carry on with your schedule.

🎬 Redesign your morning routine to include meditation/silence, exercise, journaling, gratitude and a random act of kindness. Watch as your life transforms before your very eyes. For an additional challenge, plan to do this for 30 days straight.

🎬 Get a clear view on life by grounding yourself in nature. A simple walk through the woods or time away from technology and home does the body good.

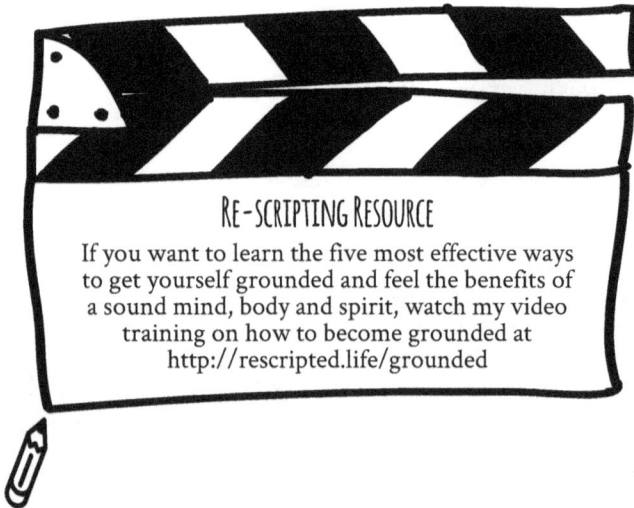

RE-SCRIPTING RESOURCE

If you want to learn the five most effective ways to get yourself grounded and feel the benefits of a sound mind, body and spirit, watch my video training on how to become grounded at
http://rescripted.life/grounded

Please Silence Your Cell Phones

> "Silence is a source of great strength."
>
> –Lao Tzu

Silence is golden. We see it quite often as we're settling in for a movie. I'm sure you value your quiet time to yourself. Speaking of which, have you checked in with yourself lately?

I have a routine of calling my grandparents when I'm on the road. Whether I'm in between planes running to the next terminal or heading back home from rowing practice, I'll give them a few minutes multiple times per week. Without fail, every time my grandmother answers the phone, she tells me she's so excited that I called, even though it's been less than 72 hours since I last called. But the greatest thing I learned from her comes at the end of the phone call. As I'm telling her that I love her and that I'll talk to her soon, she'll always say, "Take care of Zephan." She doesn't say, "Take care," or "Talk to you soon," or "Peace," like a lot of my friends do.

My grandmother reminds me that at the end of the day, I always have me, and that's a lot to care for. No matter what distractions are going on in my life or how bad my day might have been, I can always come back to me.

It's as though you're stepping into a movie theater and the lights are still on, people are filing into their seats, talking and making noise, and the ads are up on screen. There's a lot to throw you off course. You might decide now is the best time to take a bathroom break or perhaps you wanted that candy bar at the concessions despite taking five minutes to decide against it when you first walked in. Maybe some teenagers in the front of the theater are causing a scene. I know, I was always one of those kids. But at a certain point, the lights have to dim and the movie has to begin. This typically won't happen without a funny clip followed by a giant "Silence is golden" frame.

TURNING OFF DISTRACTIONS

So what distractions are going on for you, keeping you from your fullest life?

When I first quit my job, I had a lot of distractions. I woke up to my new found freedom and realized I could watch TV when I wanted, go to the fridge when I wanted or even go out for a drive or run some errands. All of this sounds like a good thing, but it isn't very conducive to a productive work day, let alone making a profit.

The first step in cutting out the distractions was changing my environment. First, I moved out of my parent's house. When I was setting up my new place, I made sure that there was a clear difference between my bed, my work space and my social spaces. A lot of the time, I would take my laptop away from my desk in my room and work at the dining room table to avoid working from bed and being lazy. But this only goes so far. It's easy to think you'll be productive when you work for yourself, but if you were to take a pen and paper and keep track of all the social media time you logged in and wasted each week, you'd be shocked.

I needed to make a change. The change of environment was good for a start, but it wasn't going to be good enough to stay home alone all day working. I began a search for an office space online, and it didn't really pan out unless I wanted to spend hundreds of dollars each month. Realistically, I probably could have afforded this if I put in some more effort, but for the sake of being frugal and getting my business off the ground, it just didn't seem right. As I searched more and more, I discovered the idea of a co-working space.

A co-working space is essentially an office building that is shared by multiple businesses. There is a shared conference room, meeting space and in many cases the working areas are open and not separated from the other businesses. It does, however, beat working from a noisy coffee house.

I found a great location that was right downtown about a mile from the waterfront, and it housed a ton of tech startups. With nearly fifty people working out of this one location, I thought surely I'd meet new potential clients and work out of an environment that cultivates creativity. Plus, it felt more like working at Google than anything, with all of the fun I saw them having.

I tried out four spaces before landing on the one I liked. The space had a full body anti-gravity massage chair, a kitchen, conference spaces, and best of all, 24/7 access. I'm not someone who jumps out of bed at seven in the morning ready to go. I thoroughly enjoy staying awake until two or three in the morning and then sleeping in until nine or so. Be sure to question yourself about your own best practices and distraction traps. Think about things like:

- What time of day am I most productive?
- What sort of scheduling framework do I work best in?
- What are some of the things I do that waste time?

Part of avoiding distractions is knowing when and how you work best. And as with many things in life, most of the time, listening to your intuition helps you make the best choices when you're determining your best practices.

The Inner Critic and the Inner Child

One of the biggest distractions I have has been with me all my life. You have it too and even if you think you don't, it's still there. Do you know what it is? It's your inner critic. He or she is the one who is sitting there on your shoulder, telling you that you'll never accomplish the big task that sits in front of you. The inner critic never sleeps and it will always have a bad attitude. You may have met some inner critics in real life.

Think of the last person that said, "Oh, you'll never be able to do that." I highly doubt you tried to think of someone and came up with nothing. There's always that one person who is so closed-minded that they'll shoot down anyone in their path.

How about the one-upper? I had the one-upper for most of my life telling me I couldn't ever do better. Any time I ever reached a high achievement, I would then realize that I could have done better and negate all the hard work I had just put in over the last significant period of time. I still do this from time to time, but now I've learned to deal with this jerk in a much more productive fashion.

I've always been the one who gets shot down and then turns around to say, "You watch me." I want to teach you how you can also develop the "Watch me" attitude. It's actually quite simple and you'll be able to start implementing this right away.

Think back to your childhood. Imagine what the house looked like, where you spent most of your time, and the toys that you had. For me, I always had Mighty Morphin Power Rangers action figures, and I would build blanket forts in the living room.

So go back to that time and find your inner child. What did you know to be true about life at that time? What restrictions were placed on you back then by the others? Were you pressured to become a doctor or lawyer? Perhaps you were raised to think that life worked in a certain way. No matter the scenario, sit there for a moment with that inner child and imagine what life was like for him or her.

The inner child is not the same as the inner voice in your head, the inner critic. The inner child was the one I visited when I had the near out-of-body experience in the float tank.

The inner voice in our heads comes from a time when we were limited. A lot of the time, I call him my inner fat kid because after I was placed on anti-depressants and gained over sixty pounds in a year, I became extremely self-conscious. My inner fat kid told me that I could never run a mile. My inner fat kid told me that I'd never amount to anything in sports because I couldn't even see my feet when I looked straight down at the ground. My inner fat kid told me that I'd never have a relationship because no one would want me.

Well, I didn't just run a mile. In fact, my first year that I started working out, my mom convinced me to sign up for a 5K race. I ran at my own pace, but I finished in forty-eight minutes. One year later, I signed up again as a reminder of what my old self accomplished. This time, I wanted to beat him, because my inner voice said it wasn't good enough. But I hit a stumbling block and the day before the race my podiatrist had to cut a hole in the bottom of my foot to remove a lump. It could have been cancer; it could have been anything, but it was devastating to hear the doctor tell me that I had to keep pressure off of my foot for a week or two.

It wasn't good enough for me to find out that I was perfectly healthy and I'd be fine in a week or two. Shocked by what was happening and dedicated to run this race, I asked him to make sure I had heard him correctly, "So does this mean I can run the 5K tomorrow?"

He scoffed and politely responded with, "You'll be lucky if you can walk tomorrow." I was desperate for an alternative and dedicated to running this race to prove that I was no longer the fat kid. I had worked so hard to turn my inner critic into an inner cheerleader, and this was the last thing I needed in my way.

The next morning, I showed up to the startling line, limping and in excruciating pain. I doubled up on socks to try and ease the pressure on the bottom of my foot, but it wasn't doing me any good. One foot in front of the other I thought. "This is one of the dumbest choices I've ever made," I muttered. But then...

The first few steps had me in agony and the first half mile was like a death march, but I stayed with the pack. After the first mile, I caught a runner's high and the pain was so excruciating that I couldn't really feel my foot anymore. I had to keep going. I barely hobbled through the finish line just thirty minutes after the starting pistol fired. My pain was gone because I channeled a new voice in my head that gave me the strength to keep going. I finished the race. I felt good enough for a few minutes.

I'm going to make a disclaimer here. I am no doctor and in no way am I giving you medical advice. I would never recommend running the day after surgery. In fact, I was foolish to even consider it, but I don't regret pushing myself past my inner voice.

But as I passed through the finish line, I looked up to note my time. I had completed the race sixteen minutes faster than the previous year. I was no longer Zephan, the fat kid. I had become Zephan, the champion, and get me to a doctor, kid, because my white socks were now soaked red and I don't think it was from the fruit they had waiting at the finish line.

You might be wondering what it takes to get yourself so fired up and so motivated that you become unstoppable. My mentor and author of Provoking Greatness, Misti Burmeister says, "At the end of the day, the only person who can help you discover what fires you up is you. And the first thing to do, if you're in a place where you just don't know, get curious and get into action. Go to something you've never gone to before. Go learn a skill you've never learned before. Take a class that you would never think would be something—you're just kind of interested in it. When I got stuck, it was farming that interested me. And I struggled so hard with letting myself be interested in farming. Like... 'I gotta focus on bigger things like leadership and like helping people grow! What is this farming thing?!' But wouldn't you know, that not even a year later, I got the chance to learn a lot about how food is grown. That was pretty exciting and fun and that's what turned my lights back on. But you've got to stay curious. You got to stay open. You've got to keep learning."

For me, fitness was something that turned the lights back on. I was overweight and the doctors were telling me my cholesterol and triglycerides were high—both indicators of heart disease, among other problems later in life. But I started to learn a new skill and all the sudden it was as if a switch was flipped.

So what was the secret about understanding who your inner child is? How did I take that inner critic voice that told me I'm fat, I'm lazy, I'm not athletic and turn it into one that enabled me to complete a half-marathon mud run, lose sixty pounds in one summer, compete on four college sports club teams and hold meaningful relationships?

Have you ever seen a kid in the grocery store who is just losing it and throwing a tantrum? You'll see one of two things happen on the parenting end with this type of situation. Either the parent does the wrong thing and starts yelling or smacking the child, sometimes threatening to take away dinner or a toy. Or, you'll see the parent who does the right thing and calmly asks, "What's wrong?"

There's a key step in this process of asking the child that will happen almost every single time. The parent gets down to the eye level of the child before asking. See, you have to get down to the eye level of your inner critic or your inner child and ask them calmly, "Hey, what's wrong? Why are you acting like this?" And when they get respectful attention, they can communicate. Remember what my grandmother always said, take care of you.

By talking it through with yourself and taking good care of you, the inner critic and the distractions all start to seem so insignificant. And the inner child can offer his or her sage wisdom of innocence, from the time in your youth before the inner critic got so noisy and demanding.

We're going to have distractions both on the outside and the inside, it's just a matter of figuring out how to talk it through and really get to the meat of what is bothering you. Once you find out both what is bothering you and how you can extinguish this issue, you'll find that you've learned a lot of new skills and become quite fond of your new attitude.

It's really hard to enjoy a movie in the theater with a lot of noise. It's hard to focus on life when there are so many distractions and inner voices. If you start to tune out what's important and maybe a little while later try to jump back in, it may be hard to tell what's going on now. Try to stay level-headed by listening to your inner child and the inner critic. Sometimes all you need to do to get someone to shut up is to just listen.

This chapter was all about your inner critic and how you can overcome those inner tantrums that get thrown from time to time. It's not easy to overpower this voice and hear your quieter inner child. Right about now you might be thinking that this change will never happen for you. The inner voice is trying to speak up and resist the changes that are already happening within your mind. It's OK to feel this way, but you have to listen to the perseverance and passion. Try to find out what new thing you can learn so that it may learn from you.

In chapter five, we'll talk about what might have been possibly the scariest experience in my life and the seven steps I deployed right away so that when the shit hits the fan, you can keep calm and carry on.

LIFE RE-SCRIPTED ACTION STEPS

- Take a day of silence and observe as much as you can. Perhaps take note in your journal of the things that surprised you. If you have to talk to people at work, keep it conservative or tell them you have a sore throat. It's just a day.
- Bonus points if you ask a friend or relative to sit with you in silence for 10 minutes. Stare into each other's eyes and be there in the moment.
- Plan out a week-long tech detox. This might be hard with work so adjust as needed but place your phone on Do Not Disturb every day and avoid social media outside of work by going for a walk or finding a new hobby.
- Design your inner child avatar in your journal. Write out what he or she looks like, what they enjoy doing, their fears and ultimately what they aspire to do.
- Research and build a list of 10 affirmations you can read out loud each morning. Be sure to include affirmations for gratitude, confidence, success and more.

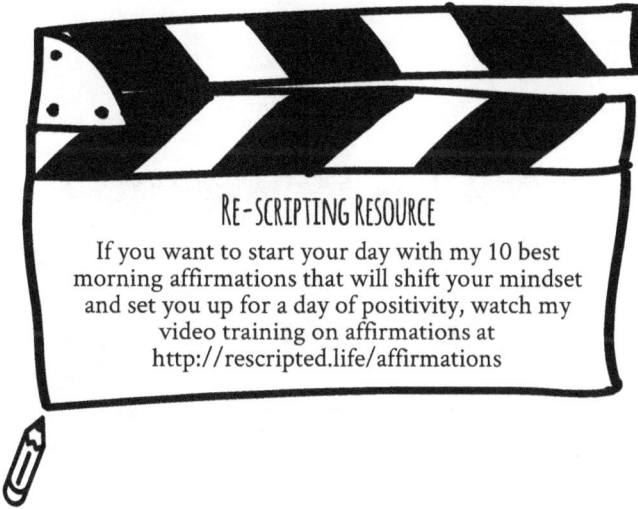

Re-scripting Resource

If you want to start your day with my 10 best morning affirmations that will shift your mindset and set you up for a day of positivity, watch my video training on affirmations at http://rescripted.life/affirmations

The Following Preview
Has Been Approved
for All Audiences

"Trade your expectation for appreciation and the world changes instantly."

–Tony Robbins

We've talked about choosing the type of genre for your movie and buying the ticket. We've moved past the concession stand and gathered your three P's to enhance the movie-watching experience, and you even picked the best seat in the house. The inner critic is at peace for now and the previews have begun.

One of the first slides that you see going into a movie is the infamous green backdrop with white text stating, The Following Preview Has Been Approved For All Audiences, courtesy of the Motion Picture Association of America.

The previews display just before a movie begins. They're a hint as to what will be coming up in the next three to six months. But they have to be good enough to keep you hanging on the edge of your seat whispering to your fellow movie-goer, "I've got to see that." Perhaps the worst part about the previews is not the fact that the movie is taking too long to begin, but more the fact that your expectations are getting set extremely high.

Think about it. You came in to watch a drama or a comedy, but you got bombarded with clips from the next James Bond installment or even worse, you find out they're remaking Star Wars for the third time. More often than not, you'll be giddy with excitement for those movies to come out, so naturally you are getting all hyped before your story has even begun.

So what happens when the story doesn't quite play out as expected? What happens when someone strays from the script, or even more important, what happens when the whole script strays from the script?

In August of 2015, I flew out to Los Angeles for work. I had a video shoot scheduled in West Hollywood and being a travel hacker, I had gotten a flight from Baltimore to LA for just $5.60. I packed my bags on a Wednesday morning and began the nine-hour journey with a layover in the middle. Arriving in California was a breeze, and eventually I worked my way over to my hotel.

After I checked in at the hotel, I did the normal things like logging into the Wi-Fi and checking out the mini-fridge to see what drinks they had stocked. I took a moment to make a motivational video I was going to post on the social media page for my podcast listeners. Things seemed normal, just like any other event I had gone out of town for, but little did I know, my story was on the verge of spiraling out of control.

A few hours later, I began the video shoot in the hotel, and it only took about forty minutes for things to go south. I started getting emails saying my email passwords had been changed and my email was being used to log in to a computer that was 3,000 miles away. Because I had used my email in Baltimore, and then here I was later that evening using my email on the West Coast, I didn't think anything of it. I went back to work.

It's great that we have a lot of technology in place to secure us, and I thought my email provider was just being cautious and it was probably nothing. But it very quickly turned into a nightmare.

My script was no longer being written by me. I later found out that it was being determined by a guy named Rocky in the Dominican Republic who had just ordered new brake rotors for his car off of my eBay account, and a shiny new cell phone from my Amazon account. He sent his cousins in New York thousands of dollars in wire transfers as well, and to round it all off, he took out a financing loan for a couple of laptops. I felt helpless and trapped seeing this, and you'll see why in a moment. The story was no longer up to me. Or so I thought.

The preview for this upcoming movie was terrorizing to say the least. There were a lot of dangers and twists those first few minutes alerted me to. But nothing could have prepared me for the full feature.

More time passed, and at one point I was on my phone, finally reading these emails to see what was going on. My phone turned to a black screen with an Apple logo and a progress bar slowly working its way across the screen.

From my time working at the Genius Bar at the Apple Store, I knew exactly what was happening. My phone was being remotely erased by someone who had accessed my cloud account and used the lost/stolen feature to secure the phone. Immediately, my heart sank, I began to perspire and my hands got clammy.

Here I was, the former "genius" and I was losing all of my technology and access to the outside world in a matter of seconds, all while being 3,000 miles away from home. The pencil was working its way feverishly across the page, erasing my expectation of how this movie would play out and re-writing what would have been considered a "feel good" movie of the year and turned it into a bone chilling horror flick.

Originally I had worked out my trip so I could fly to Los Angeles, film that evening, then move over to an Airbnb that was run out of a co-working space. I could work from there for three days until I flew out to Denver, Colorado, to stay with my best friend, whom I consider a brother, for my birthday. I had this whole plan in place and I wanted it all to stay on the path I had dictated. I set an expectation and I placed the bar really high.

There's a big difference between a goal and an expectation. Merriam-Webster defines a goal as something you are trying to do or achieve. An expectation is a belief that something will happen or is likely to happen. The former is the outcome you are working towards whereas the latter is the way in which you expect that outcome to occur. I'm not saying you shouldn't place the bar high, I'm saying you need to keep a reasonable expectation. Sometimes things don't go as planned and you need to be prepared for that.

So when you find that your script is being shifted beyond your control, it's your intuition that will keep you grounded in scenarios like mine. Here are the steps I recommend that you take:

- Accept that factors beyond your control are changing.
- Turn to your basic needs
- Determine the best course of action
- See the course through to your highest ability
- Take time to decompress
- Examine your story and accept it
- Determine your new story and go

Back to the disaster. Since I was on a job for a client, and since I held myself to a certain quality standard, I had to show him I wasn't fazed. I calmly explained the situation to him and he was extremely understanding. He offered to let me borrow his phone and computer to do what I had to do.

After realizing that things were beyond my control, I kept going to think to myself, "Ok, what do I need to do right now, for food, shelter, water, *etc.*" I ran to the hotel ATM to take out the max amount of cash, which turned out to be a measly two-hundred dollars. I figured worst case, it would get me a burner phone from a local electronics store, or food for the next couple days. That was really what I cared about—my basic needs.

I wouldn't quite consider a phone a basic need, but it certainly helps in a country that constantly depends on technology. We don't even have pay phones anymore so it would take a bit of resourcefulness if I had to contact someone once I left the hotel.

So there I was with $200 in cash, no phone or email, and I assumed my laptop sitting up in my hotel room would be useless when I got back. The lovely thing about being connected to the cloud is that not only is your information stored there, but should you need to erase it all and kill your devices in one foul swoop, it's quite easy. Despite having a comfy air conditioned hotel room and a client who was more than accommodating, I had to figure out what my next steps were.

I was very fortunate that whomever had compromised my accounts had not yet touched my laptop. Some quick thinking ensued and I turned off the Wi-Fi, thereby disconnecting from the Internet. If someone had sent a signal through to my computer to wipe it, it wasn't happening that day. I had a flash drive on me so I backed up all the important files to it since there was a good chance the Mac could still get erased. Oddly enough, the first draft of this book was on that laptop, and it was my only copy. Funny how things work out.

I got my backup unplugged and stowed away with my personal items so it would stick with me the rest of the trip. Then I jumped back onto the Internet, thinking, *I've got to get myself out of here and figure out what is happening.* My heart was beating faster and my irises were glued to the screen, as if a new 007 movie was being announced. I thought at that point that my computer was the best tool to use. I could attempt to recover my email, which would allow me into my cloud account, which in turn would let me get my iPhone back up and running. Sweet.

While the phone reset, I logged onto Facebook and recorded a video explaining everything that I experienced that day. At first I saw it as a way to get my stress out, because if other people knew what I was going through, maybe I'd feel better about my situation. Just as the video was uploaded 100%, the computer started wiping itself. The phone wiped itself again, and in the blink of an eye, my whole life went down the drain.

The course of action at this point was to get to safety. It was clearly not in the cards for me to stay in California, so I needed to get home as soon as humanly possible. It would suck to cancel the rest of my trip, especially my birthday with my friend, but it was the smartest choice in my eyes at the time.

So how do you get a flight home if you have just been disconnected from everything? Never doubt the power of asking for help from the hotel lobby assistant. Within the short forty-five seconds it took me to take the elevator down to the lobby and no more than thirty seconds to explain my story, I was on a computer booking a flight home. This is where some smart thinking needed to come into play because my credit cards at this point were all frozen and I could have easily been trapped.

Keeping calm under pressure is so crucial. When you let your panic get the better of you, you start to think illogically. But if you can keep it under control, you can see the new story through to the end.

Street smarts knocked on the door and reminded me I had sky miles points, and, worst case scenario, I could ask a friend on Facebook using the hotel computer to buy me a ticket if the first plan failed. My first break came when I logged into my American Airlines account and found the 100,000 sky miles I had socked away. I had planned on using those for a trip to Thailand, but now was not the time to think about that.

I booked a flight home for the next morning, and called it a night. There was nothing more to be done that day. I could finish my client work in the morning before getting a cab to the airport.

I flirted with a passenger on my layover and found out she was from my hometown. I asked to borrow her phone to call my parents and beg for a ride home from the airport at two in the morning. In my daze through the whole situation I failed to realize I had booked first class seats on both legs of the flight home, which was the silver lining of it all: free drinks and meals and the comfort of a lay-flat bed and microfiber blanket.

I didn't know to decompress after the whole situation but after everything happened, I took a few days to just be alone. I didn't talk to many people other than a quick update to my friends on social media. I skipped going out with friends to sit inside and watch Netflix. My body and my mind naturally knew that I had to chill out for a bit. Think about it, when your plans get pummeled that bad, it makes sense to take it easy and ice down your bruises.

On the third day, I woke up and had a little check-in with myself. I asked questions about whether or not my basic needs were being met, which they were, and double checked that I felt safe. When the mind agreed that I was back in good hands, it released me from the burden of silence and opened me up to recover. I started sharing my story with my friends, playing back every detail in my head as they questioned me how it could have happened.

I analyzed each moment and walked through it repeatedly to see if I could have done anything better. I loved that I put my client first and told him I would deliver every service I had promised. I thanked myself for staying calm in a high-stress situation. I appreciated that

77

I took all the right steps to get through the painful events that had transpired and found the ability to be grateful that it happened to me because I wouldn't wish it upon anyone else.

The only thing you can do when you have set an expectation of what the future will look like is to take each moment as it happens. The movie won't always look as good as the preview did. Remember, they're taking a two-hour film and condensing it into two minutes. But who says the story has to end there? It's up to you whether or not you'll keep going back to the movies, but if you didn't show up in the first place, you wouldn't have seen the previews.

I interviewed J Massey, who went from rock bottom to real estate investor, and I just wanted to tell you his quick story about how he turned a situation around when he had an expectation for how his story should play out. After leaving his career as a financial planner to learn real estate, and upon finding himself broke, squatting in his own house how he had lost possession of, with his pregnant wife, he had this happen...

"So I went to go play volleyball, because I was trying to blow off some steam. I thought that was gonna help. I jumped, landed on a guy's head, punctured my lung, and now I couldn't walk or talk without fainting. So, if you can imagine, I'm learning a new industry that I've never done before. I'm unable to walk or talk simultaneously without fainting. My wife can't eat or drink. And we have no money. And that's the situation.

"With kids in tow. So you've gotta understand that that was our situation, and what makes me work and do the things that I do today. When you're fighting for something as basic as clothing, food, and shelter, and you're really clear on that—well, you get to work and you make a lot of things happen."

Your expectations will come and go, and watching the previews of a movie will set a lot of expectations. The ultimate question, though, is whether or not you'll give it a chance and go see the movie despite bad reviews.

I challenge you to blow past your expectations and just appreciate the circumstances. In chapter six, it's time to start the show. I know that it feels like the movie took forever to get started and that's usually what people think during the previews. They're waiting for the lights to go down, they're waiting for the movie to start and sometimes it takes longer than you would think. There you go setting those expectations again!

So what will you do with your time now that each second is available for you to experience? No more waiting, let's start the show.

Life Re-Scripted Action Steps

- Build a chain of protocol that you can follow when the script sways. No matter if it involves crying over a gallon of ice cream or going for a run, know what you should do in times of crisis.
- Lower your expectations from time to time. Ouch really? Yes! Expectations are the root of all heartache so practice lowering the bar for yourself. When you rocket past the metaphorical bar, give yourself a pat on the back for your accomplishment. Stop beating yourself up.

- 🎞 Share your expectations with others. If no one else knows what you expect of them, how can they behave in the manner you were hoping?

- 🎞 Accept what is true in this moment. Every day might not be a good day but there is a silver lining in each and every experience of our lives.

- 🎞 Find your reset button so that you can dig yourself out of any bad day. Determine what the one thing is that will always leave you in a good mood. What is the one thing you can do to get back up and running 100% as quickly as possible?

RE-SCRIPTING RESOURCE

If you want to learn how to hit the reset button and start over so that you can rapidly rise out of a bad day, watch my video training on how to hit the reset button at http://rescripted.life/reset

Enjoy the Show

"Life's like a movie, write your own ending. Keep believing, keep pretending."

–Jim Henson

Have you ever been afraid of missing out on all that life has to offer? Or, have you ever been watching TV or a movie, and you dazed out for what felt like just a moment and then you realized you missed the whole first half? What were you doing in that time? I've done it while in the car driving from place to place. I won't remember stopping at the last four red lights in spite of the fact I know I waited for them to turn green.

I just want to make sure you are in the right mindset so life doesn't pass you by. This chapter is all about being present and ensuring your experience is one hundred percent authentic. At the end I'll show you some interesting numbers on how we spend our time.

Now you've come down from the adrenaline high of watching the coming attractions, the lights dim a bit more and it's time to settle in. The movie of your life is just beginning. When you get started with the movie, it takes a little bit before you understand what's going on. In many cases, you only know what the two minute trailer told you and that's just the tip of the iceberg.

But very soon you are about to discover some life-changing things for your main character. You'll be introduced to the big obstacle our hero must overcome. There might be a love interest or two and a lot of struggle along the way.

This isn't a dress rehearsal, this is the real deal. A big fear of mine is I'll go through life so stuck in my own head, that I'll miss out on the experiences happening right before my very eyes. How many times have you been in conversation with someone, but your phone buzzes, you look down to text someone back and next thing you know, you've missed the last five minutes of the conversation?

I have to admit something—I've done this to so many people that I've lost count. Or I'll enter my own little world so to speak and minutes will go by. I'll hear the murmur of the conversation going on and perhaps add in a "yea" or "uh-huh" here and there to make it seem like I'm paying attention, but in reality I've checked out a long time ago.

It's frightening how much we miss by doing this; I mean what would happen if you were driving on the highway and just checked out completely? What if you had a very precision job in a machine shop and were working with a power tool and just dazed off into la-la land? You could lose a finger, a hand, or worse, your life. Checking out is dangerous and in the case of watching a movie while not life threatening, it can definitely suck to miss the good parts.

Tech Detox

One thing I recommend to my friends when they feel bogged down by social media or technology is to take a tech detox. It was hard for me when I first started doing this, but my identity theft crisis really tested my faith. Here I was back at the airport having a whole day of travel ahead of me, my music was gone because my phone had been hacked, and it was the middle of the day, so sleeping on the plane wasn't going to happen. I bought two two-hundred page books and I managed to finish both of them in a day. That's more reading than I do in a month!

So how do you go about creating a super productive environment and purging yourself of unwanted distractions so you can enjoy the show?

One of the things I've tried is the float tank experience. A float tank is a lightproof, soundproof tank filled with about six inches of water and 1000 lbs of Epsom salt. Just an hour in this tank while staying conscious is so relaxing that it takes your mind off of everything going on. You don't have to do anything this drastic, but anything that gets you away from work and life for a little while can be extremely beneficial.

Another thing I do is if I have a set schedule for myself is to set my phone to Do Not Disturb, because I already have a plan for the day and I don't need any interruptions, a.k.a. other people's agendas, getting in the way. This allows me to stick to the plan. If it's really an emergency, I'll find out because I can check my phone in between tasks, but otherwise, I remind myself that whatever it is can wait.

If you're feeling hyper ambitious, you could take a three or four day retreat and turn your phone off the entire time. In Spring of 2015, I took a trip with my rowing crew to a training camp to spend four days on an old plantation, living in a bed and breakfast and training with some of the best coaches in the world.

From 6 am until 9 pm we were rowing thirty to forty-five kilometers a day on a private lake. That's nearly thirty miles a day. It was the perfect time for me to put technology aside, turn on an email vacation responder and just enjoy the weekend.

It was hard at first, leaving my phone in the room, but it was rewarding to be able to experience each and every moment. From the jokes to the home-cooked meals, this trip was a great way to reset my mind. I stopped getting phantom vibrations in my pocket making me think my phone was going off, only to realize it wasn't in my pocket.

No one on their deathbed is going to say, "I wish I would have worked more," or "I wish I had spent more time on the phone texting people." The experience is all happening on screen right here in front of you so let me leave you with this…

The average American will live 28,835 days. The first fifteen years of your life comes out to 5,475 days, which leaves you with 23,360 days left in your adult life.

On average you will:
- Sleep for 8,477 days
- Prepare food for 1,635 days
- Be at work for 3,202 days

- Commute or travel for 1,099 days
- Watch television (on average) for 2,676 days
- Complete household activities for 1,576 days
- Care for the needs of others like friends and family for 564 days
- Spend 671 days bathing, grooming and doing bathroom activities
- Participate in community activities like taking classes or volunteering for charity for 720 days
- You are left with 2740 days or roughly seven and a half years.

What are you going to do with the time that remains? If you knew that you only had seven years left to your life, wouldn't you want to change how you've been spending it? Will you spend those years sitting back passively watching the movie play out in front of you, but not really stepping up to be a part of it? Or will you train yourself to be present and in the moment so that you can enjoy all that life has to offer?

What if you got down to day zero and you had twenty-four hours left? Would everything that has lead up to this exact moment make you feel fulfilled about your life story?

The fictitious movie character Ferris Bueller states, "Life moves pretty fast, if you don't stop and look around once and a while, you could miss it." Truer words haven't been spoken, Mister Bueller.

I live my life by that quote and I'm sure it has you thinking about how often you "check out" from your daily life. It's easy to do so when you aren't living in alignment with your passions. But the great news is that you can start aligning with your passions by picking and choosing exactly who should be a part of your life. You'll decide on a director, producer, writer, editor and even the casting manager.

This is what the next chapter is about. It's a choice but it's completely up to you. It all starts with deciding who is in charge of the show. So without further ado, here are the opening credits.

Life Re-Scripted Action Steps

- Improve your relationship with money by taking control of your finances. Understand what experiences you can or cannot do at this time but set your goals on an experience that you would like in the next year.

- Check in with yourself by setting reminders on your phone. Use a service like EmailFuture.com or Boomerang Inbox to send yourself emails during a busy time reminding you to take a break. Use Calm.com if you need a quick break too.

- Stop and smell the roses. Once again, nature has a huge impact on our mind, body and spirit. Try taking your shoes off and standing on the grass for ten minutes to ground your energy and connect with something bigger than yourself.

- Script the perfect last day of your life. If you had unlimited resources and time to spend your last day on earth, how would you spend it? Know what a life well spent means to you.

- Beat FOMO (fear of missing out) by being still. Stop, take a moment and just be here in this very second.

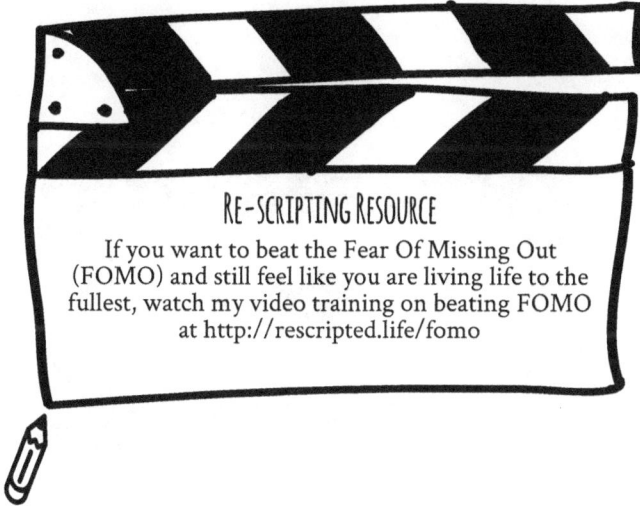

Re-scripting Resource

If you want to beat the Fear Of Missing Out (FOMO) and still feel like you are living life to the fullest, watch my video training on beating FOMO at http://rescripted.life/fomo

The Opening Credits

"When I was a kid, there was no collaboration; it's you with a camera bossing your friends around. But as an adult, film-making is all about appreciating the talents of the people you surround yourself with and knowing you could never have made any of these films by yourself."

–Steven Spielberg

This chapter is one that I'm always a bit hesitant to write about because it's going to require you to be selective about who belongs in your life. I'll prompt you with some important questions that will help you determine, this but a brief warning: this part isn't for the faint of heart.

When I first started on my entrepreneurial journey, I had to make some big choices that I'll share with you in this chapter, choices that impacted my mentality and aspirations for success.

One of the first things that I learned the night that I decided to leave my corporate job was that I would now be responsible for surrounding myself with a better crowd. You'll have to make the same kinds of choices while you re-script your life. While some of these decisions might hurt at first or seem impossible to make, I promise you that keeping track of where you spend your time and who you spend it with will be one of the best decisions you make.

The opening credits to a movie typically start out with the name of the studio, the production company, and go on to share the name of the director, producer and the writer. But more importantly, this is where the principal actors are advertised.

You've probably heard the saying that you are the sum of the five people you surround yourself with the most. This lesson was crucial to my success both in business and in life. I started to take a look around after I quit my job to examine with whom I was spending the most of my time with.

As it turns out, I was still spending my weekends with most of my high school buddies, not really accomplishing much of anything. This isn't to say that they were bad people, but time with them certainly wasn't going to be conducive to reaching my goals. It wasn't time for a breakup. It was just time to switch the starring actors to less important roles.

It doesn't matter what change you are looking to make in your life, but whatever it is, you need to be sure to spend your journey with those that have already accomplished it. Do you want to lose weight?

You probably won't manage it if you keep going out to dinner with your friends who always go to the Italian restaurant and hobble out when they are done each week.

Looking to build a successful business? Spend more time around entrepreneurs and successful business owners who have been there and done that.

Take a moment to sit back and think about your friends, your family, coworkers and any acquaintances you might run into. Anyone you meet, really, but these are people that you see more than once in your life. Now consider last weekend, where were you? Who were you with? I'm not trying to interrogate you or make you feel guilty about some of your choices of companion. I'm simply recommending you be more conscious of those you spend the most time with.

And who are you signing on as the director and producer of your story? How about the writer or the editor?

That's a trick question, because the truth is, you are the director, the producer, the writer and the editor. If you haven't figured it out, right now you are in charge of your own destiny and you are at a unique crossroads.

You could take what I've taught so far and say, "Thanks, this all sounds quite interesting but I'm really not sure I have the grit to make it through." But something tells me if you've read this far, you don't want to fail at this because this is your last shot to start living life on your own terms.

I'd like to share with you a simple trick that I call the Life-Casting Principle. The Life-Casting Principle states that your life story and the success and happiness included within it is directly correlated to the happiness and success of the people you cast in the supporting roles of your life.

You see, it's all up to you, really. It always has been.

Life-Casting Your Life

Here's a quick questionnaire I've created that will help you determine the seven people you should spend the most time with:

- Who is the one person that you know who is constantly striving to develop himself or herself through learning and experimentation?
- Who is the one person who embodies success and is waking up every day to either a career or a business that he or she is absolutely in love with?
- Who is the one person who is best at keeping track of his or her finances, knowing when to spend (or invest) and has enough money to suit their dreams?
- Who is the one person who treats their family members with the utmost respect and compassion despite anything going on in their life?
- Who is the one person who always has a smile on his or her face, can spark up a conversation with anyone, and always knows someone when asked for help?
- Who is the one person who has mastered the art of loving his or her body, and goes the extra mile to provide his or herself with the proper nutrition and fitness?
- Who is the one person who takes time alone without interruption to check in, feel gratitude and ultimately has a warming and peaceful aura?

Congratulations! You've just found the seven people that you need to start surrounding yourself with the most. Now if you went through this exercise and thought one of the answers was someone you might not ever be able to meet I have a little dare for you.

I dare you to contact them. Go ahead and find their website or social media page and send them a message, a tweet, a snail mail right now. I don't care what it is, but try.

When I left my job in 2013, I immediately wrote to someone that I looked up to—it was Pat Flynn of the *Smart Passive Income Blog*. After being laid off from his architect position, he started teaching himself how to blog for money and ultimately went on to teach others how to run a successful online business. In the email, I explained to him that I took the leap and how I had been following him for years. I told him that his story inspired me, because I thought if this guy did it, maybe I could, too.

He wrote back to me, saying, "A lot of people go into something and stick with it, only to realize it's not what they should have done in the first place. For me, it took getting laid off to finally realize that—a huge blessing in disguise. For you, you discovered that on your own early and although things are scary, exciting, ecstatic and confusing all at the same time right now, your older self will look back on this time of your life and thank you for it."

I had never met him in person, and I thought "Why would someone with such a following, with such stature, care about a little guy like me?" The coolest thing was two years later, after I had built a successful video production company and podcast, I got to meet him in person. Never doubt who you can connect with.

As my old employer Bill Glazer once said, "Don't ask, don't get."

So back to this whole Life-Casting Principle, because it wouldn't be very successful if we didn't talk about the star role. In *X-Men*, they cast

Hugh Jackman to play Wolverine; in *Batman,* Christian Bale was cast to play Bruce Wayne. These actors weren't chosen just because they were good at acting. They were picked because they suited the part.

Wolverine is meant to be a jacked, hairy beast, and Batman is supposed to be this suave billionaire by day. These guys fit those personas. Are you trying to live out a role that doesn't suit who you really are? Are you being truthful to yourself and your inner desires?

I've seen movies that have tons of great actors in them, but the stories still sucked. And I've seen movies with no-names that have an amazing plot. It's all about getting the right person for the right role. Review the Life-Casting questionnaire and think long and hard about the people you want in your life.

Then go ahead and turn it around to find out who no longer serves your journey. Think about things like:

- Who is the one person you know who is NOT constantly striving to develop himself or herself through learning and experimentation?
- Who is the one person who DOES NOT embody success and is CONSTANTLY COMPLAINING about his business or career?
- Who is the one person who is THE WORST at keeping track of her finances and is CONSTANTLY FLUCTUATING in and out of debt?
- Who is the one person who treats his family members DISRE-SPECTFULLY and is only concerned about himself?
- Who is the one person who IS NEVER talking to people and only goes to others when it best serves her own agenda?
- Who is the one person who has NOT taken care of himself and hates to workout and eat healthy?

🎞 Who is the one person who NEVER takes time for herself and gives too much of herself to others, leaving nothing for their own sanity?

You see how easy it can be to understand who to cast as characters for your new life, right?

By simply understanding that you have the largest role as director, producer, editor, writer and casting manager, you've now eliminated everyone else from that role.

No one else should be dictating your life or how it should play out. Let me remind you of my video editing professor, who taught me to turn chicken shit into chicken salad. You have this ability; you always have had it. You just might not have realized it, but the power is there. It's time to change who you surround yourself with. Get the right part of the chicken.

In the next chapter I'm going to share with you my biggest secret for success no matter what aspect of life I'm concerned with. It's time for the movie to transition into Act One.

🎬

Life Re-Scripted Action Steps

🎞 Use the activities described above to determine the people in your life that are no longer serving you. This isn't to say you need to write them a breakup letter but stay aware of your surroundings. Don't spend time with people that hold you back.

🎞 Reach out and connect with three people that you look up to that you don't think will respond. You'd be surprised who might turn up when you take a risk. Whether it be a famous author or a speaker than you resonate with, look them up online and send a simple, "Hello, you made a difference in my life."

- Find a mentor, someone you highly respect, who will take you under their wing and provide you the necessary training and education to reach your highest potential.

- Design your ideal tribe. These are the three people that will have the maximum impact on your life and provide the most support to you in your journey.

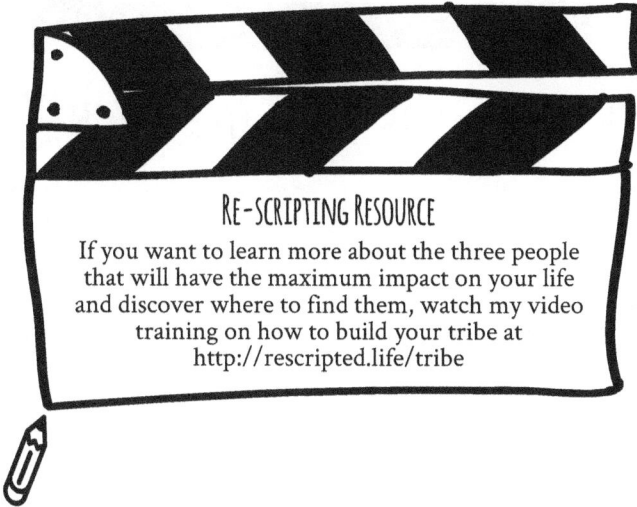

RE-SCRIPTING RESOURCE

If you want to learn more about the three people that will have the maximum impact on your life and discover where to find them, watch my video training on how to build your tribe at http://rescripted.life/tribe

Act One: The 5X Life Hack Rule

"If you want to view paradise, simply look around and view it. Anything you want to, do it. Want to change the world? There's nothing to it."

–Willy Wonka

At this point, you probably have a better perspective on who is in your life and what your life would look like if it were sprawled out on paper like a movie script. You know the three P's that can enhance your life: patience, passion and perseverance.

You are also armed with the knowledge of a casting manager because it is up to you who gets to share in your life. Much like Willy Wonka said, though; this is it. If you are waiting for life to start, stop waiting, because it's right here happening every second. It's unfolding in front of your very eyes like a projector on a screen. The only difference is this projector doesn't stop. There is no pause.

Welcome to the main event, the first act. The rising action has all led up to this one superior moment in time in which you will take a new direction in your life re-scripted. I didn't really know that I could change the story of my life until I had seen what was possible. Some of the time, we'll witness others do it and on occasion we'll do it ourselves, only to look back in shock that we were able to accomplish such a feat.

Looking back now since I started on this very peculiar journey, I can see that the last year of my life has been all about living it to the fullest and making the most out of each situation. I've laughed, I've cried, I've laughed until I cried and everything in between.

Never in my life did I imagine I would have traveled to twenty-five states in less than twelve months without paying more than six dollars in taxes for a plane ticket. I didn't think that I would build a business with clients who trusted me enough to ship me and my video gear all the way across the country just to work with them. I didn't think I could take a whole month off from working to re-analyze where my life was. I thought that I would come home from that month broke and be forced to move out onto the streets. I was wrong.

Nothing moves until you do, which is exactly why I want to share with you my 5X Life Hack Rule. This is also known as the Struggle to Hustle Golden Ratio.

Life can be really complicated, but after looking back over the accomplishments, the failures, the disappointments and the learning experiences, I found five things to be the absolute key to my success.

In an effort to be as unbiased as possible, I put them to the test to make sure this could work for anyone.

The 5X Life Hack Rule, a.k.a. 5XLHR goes as follows:

A little bit of STRUGGLE combined with the right amount of HUSTLE are the only two ingredients in EDITING your story, that lead to a LIFE that you LOVE.

Struggle

Looking back through history you'll find that every great success story involved struggle. There's always some great challenge that comes up, whether in the story of *We Are Marshall,* a movie based on a true story of a football team that tragically died in a plane crash, or *Remember the Titans,* when they're running through the Gettysburg Battlefield and they get a speech about hatred and how racism will not be tolerated.

The struggle is real. I say this quite often because we live in a world where the struggle isn't pretty. It's not attractive. You don't see people jumping onto Facebook when they hit a certain challenge in life to take photos and document what is happening. No, you see the successes, the wins, the exciting parts of life.

We all are connected on social media to that one person that just hates the universe and thinks that it is out to get them. But that struggle is self created. Have you ever noticed that it's this same person who always tends to get sick or hurt? If they added the next ingredient, they'd soon realize that it isn't all that complicated to change their life.

HUSTLE

The next part is the hustle. Gary Vaynerchuk of Vaynermedia says, "My store, Wine Library, outsells big national chains. How do you think we do it? It started with hustle. I always say that our success wasn't due to my hundreds of online videos about wine that went viral, but to the hours I spent talking to people online afterward, making connections and building relationships."

No one ever became successful without hustle and if you are sitting there thinking that the lottery winners never had to put in any hard work, check out this statistic:

The National Endowment for Financial Education cites research estimating that 70 percent of people who suddenly receive a large sum of money will lose it within a few years.

Oops... back to square one. It all comes back to the struggle and the hustle. Your success will be directly correlated to the balance of struggle and hustle. If you are thrown every obstacle in the book and you decide halfway through that you don't want to hustle as hard, the success will not follow. I'm no superman. I'm not any different from you. I'm just a guy who decided to embrace the suck for a shorter period of time than most (despite it being exponentially tougher), because I know that success is on the other side of this great big thing that one day I'll look back and call a journey.

Editing

The next part of 5XLHR is editing your story. Through all your pain, agony and struggle there is a story to be told. Whether or not you think you can change the outcome, you can.

After movies are written, sometimes they'll get to filming and they'll cut entire scenes out of the script. Some of them might be re-written and others just get thrown in the trash.

When I was feeling dissatisfied about my story for too long, here's what I did… and I highly recommend you do this, too.

One day I grabbed a legal notepad. It's just like any other piece of lined paper but it's a bit longer so there is more room to write. I cracked open a beer and sat down on the couch for a few hours and just put my pen to paper. I wrote down everything I knew to be true about myself at that moment in time from my financials to my physical activity. I even wrote down where I had traveled and the connections I had made this year. Later on in this book you'll get a chance to do so but for now, just bear with me.

After sitting there for nearly two hours, I had a fully written script of my life. Essentially, this was my life on paper and how I felt it looked to others. The key here is to make sure you write down everything you know to be true. This isn't the time to figure out what you want out of life. You've got to start somewhere and the best place is starting here, in this moment.

Once you've exhausted all facts and you have a complete blueprint of who you think you are, then and only then can you continue to expand and grow.

So I'd like for you to pause for a bit here in the book and do the following:

The Life-Scripting Exercise

Grab yourself a notebook, a legal pad or a big piece of paper and start writing down everything you know to be true about the following categories of your life:

- ⚙ Mental/learning/personal development
- ⚙ Vocational/career/business
- ⚙ Financial
- ⚙ Family
- ⚙ Social
- ⚙ Physical
- ⚙ Spiritual

Don't leave out a single detail. Write all day if you have to, but make sure you get this out and on paper. This isn't something you should do on the computer—there's something about the physical act of your brain putting ink to paper that creates a deeper understanding. Simply put, it won't have the proper effect on you if you type this, so just suck it up and write it out.

Once you've taken the time it takes to do this well, you can move on to the next chapter, which is all about determining where to go next.

But first, I have to tell you about Ronsley Vaz because he truly understands how to be thankful for the things that he does have. Ronsley is an entrepreneur specializing in creating businesses that connect people and ideas in new and innovative ways. He is the host of Australia's number one food podcast, *Bond Appetit*, which focuses on two main areas: uniting entrepreneurs through food, and fixing their relationships with food.

So I asked him how it's possible to pair up a business with his passions so that he can really make a difference in the world. His answer was quite surprising. Instead of having a big dream or vision, he mentioned to me how one small act of kindness really goes a long way for him:

"I saw this homeless guy, and I don't know what happened to me, man. Like I still—I'm struggling from the emotion that I went through, but I couldn't stop crying. I mean, I've seen this before! I don't know what was different, I really don't. But it was just one of those weird experiences that I was just so grateful for being in the position that I was in.

"I just went and bought a ham and cheese croissant and went and gave it to the guy. And he's like 'No, I have some milk in my bag.' I said 'No, I just bought it for you. It's very tasty, just baked from the bakery.'

"If your business is taking someone and giving them a life that they want, on purpose, then you're making a difference. It doesn't necessarily have to be in a third world country, doesn't necessarily have to be rags to riches sort of story. I wanted to make a difference because I saw both sides of the story. So I wanted to find a way to do that."

Going into the exercise here you might realize there are a lot of things you want, but really the goal is to see what you have, what you have to work with and where to start. And it's not about changing the planet. Just help someone with something. It can start there. You don't have to ponder changing the world. It's just about doing whatever it is that you can do to make anyone's life easier. And that could be it. Your business could be doing that for someone.

So when you are going through this life-scripting exercise and writing down everything you know about yourself, don't get frustrated or disappointed by what you discover. The best part about this is that you will begin to see your foundation, where you are starting from, to build your life and turn your dream into a reality.

No one likes the music in a scary movie because it tells them when something bad is about to happen, but this happens in all movies, not just the horror flicks. I'm telling you in this movie, something really good is about to happen. I can faintly hear your song of inspiration and hope starting to play.

LIFE RE-SCRIPTED ACTION STEPS

- Accept the gift in the struggles that arrive in your life. Just like there is good in every day, there is good in every situation. Carry a token of appreciation with you that you can refer back to in times of pain and triumph like a photo or quote.
- Fail often. Part of embracing the hustle is constantly failing forward so that you can grow and become better. Dare yourself to participate in a week long rejection challenge where you ask permission to do something each day that you think will end in rejection.
- Edit your story and delay gratification with the satisfaction in knowing your gift will be even more glorious if you display patience.
- Love with an open heart. Go out and tell the one person you care about the most how much you really love them.

When a risk comes up in your life, take the leap without thinking about it for once. After you've jumped, watch where the pieces land, examine and learn from your mistakes. But don't forget to keep going.

RE-SCRIPTING RESOURCE

If you want to leverage the 5XLHR Rule also known as the struggle to hustle golden ratio in your life for an accelerated path to a purposeful life, watch my video training at
http://rescripted.life/hustle

Act Two: The Journey
of the Protagonist, Part I

"Do you wish to rise? Begin by descending. You plan a tower that will pierce the clouds? Lay first the foundation of humility."

–Saint Augustine

It's time to talk about the protagonist of the story, the main character if you will: YOU! This is your journey to take and I thought that in this chapter I could provide a quick road map for you to use on this adventure. You never really know what is going to come next, but it never hurts to have some idea of what you can expect. This is where we can look to the natural format of a superhero movie and gain some

RE-SCRIPTED

insight as to what we might expect from our obstacles, from our fears and even from our successes.

Let me be clear, this is not to set an expectation. We all know that when you set expectations, they can easily be shut down. The other thing to keep in mind is that guidelines were meant to be broken, or swayed one direction or the other.

Every great story—whether it be in the Marvel Comic world, the DC Comics universe or better yet, real life—involves a hero. Christopher Reeve, the actor who played Superman before he was permanently paralyzed in an accident said, "I think a hero is an ordinary individual who finds strength to persevere and endure in spite of overwhelming obstacles." I think we forget that every so-called "superhero" was once an ordinary person who was tasked with a seemingly impossible goal.

Climbing Out of the Cave

In the story of Bruce Wayne, a.k.a. Batman, the protagonist finds himself in a literal and metaphorical cave where he has sunk quite deep. He has lost both of his parents and at a young age, he becomes the heir to a fortune. In this cave, he is surrounded by bats (which ultimately are his biggest fear), but he faces the darkness and climbs towards the light to embrace his inner hero and save the city.

In *Spiderman*, Peter Parker loses his uncle, and in *Iron Man*, Tony Stark nearly loses his life. But the one thing that all of these stories have in common is that the main character, the hero, after hitting rock bottom, finds the will and the courage to start climbing his way out. You are no different than these characters. The reason why these stories are so powerful is because we can relate to them psychologically.

Exploring the depths of your particular cave is going to take some soul searching, and perhaps meditation is in order. One tool I found to be instrumental in my success is the Samadhi float tank that I've mentioned before. It is absolutely harmless, but you have to be willing to lie down in a tank that is about eight feet long and six feet wide. The tank gets filled with water about six inches deep and over one thousand pounds of Epsom salt. It essentially becomes the Dead Sea because you float right on top of the water except for two conditions: it's 100% soundproof and lightproof. The water gets heated to the same temperature as your body, and you just float there.

Most people don't even feel the water after a couple minutes, and it feels as if you are floating through space. The light and sound deprivation enhances your ability to fall into a deep, meditative state. Many speak of a positive hallucination that occurs as did in my experience. When I finally let go of trying to relax and just "existed," my mind almost shut off for a moment, and then it rebooted to a memory of the time when I was about five years old.

I was on the floor of the kitchen in my childhood home, naked except for a Superman cape that I used to wear. I was seeing my inner hero—the inner child that has always motivated me to stay young at heart.

As I approached him, I found an extreme calm and serenity coming over me, and I decided to ask him what I was doing there. We moved into deep questions about love and life. He answered each one as if he were ten or even twenty years older than me. He somehow knew that things were going to be just fine and this was the reassurance I needed to continue down the path I was on.

But I know that this isn't for everyone, so in an effort to make this experience of diving deep into the cave possible, I highly recommend some form of meditation or yoga. You need to get your mind to that place where it can shut off and reboot itself and start over fresh.

Most major cities have local yoga studios with a trial month offer to see if it is right for you. I also discovered a Shambhala center near my house that offers free meditations every night of the week. Shambhala takes its name from a legendary kingdom famous for being an enlightened society. Today, the global Shambhala network brings together people from all over the world to explore our inner-most thoughts, transform our lives and awaken ourselves to our highest potential.

I know this all sounds a bit odd. Reading right now, you may notice an uneasy feeling in your throat or the pit of your stomach. It's because I'm recommending things that you might not have otherwise considered and that's OK. Your mind is stuck in this place that doesn't allow you to open up.

Guys are trained to be tough macho men and when I started this journey, a lot of the things I was being asked to do required me to be vulnerable and share my story. It required me to take steps into places both mentally and physically that I could never have prepared for. But you know what else it did? It got me to where I am now. So when it comes to opening your mind and your heart to your fullest potential, you've got to explore your cave.

FINDING YOUR KRYPTONITE

What is the weakness inside that is hurting the hero fundamentally—very deeply? In the movies, solving this problem is what the entire story is going to revolve around. It's not much different in real life. The way you are going to solve it is by going after a particular goal, and by going after it, you will be overcoming your great internal weakness.

Many people have more than one weakness, and personal weaknesses change over time, so in this very moment you must determine what is your current kryptonite.

At one point, panic attacks were my kryptonite. They were debilitating and I succumbed to the feelings—giving up and hiding away from the world. At thirteen, I had lost a friend to bullying and suicide, and another to a car accident. My life was crumbling around me and I felt like I couldn't breathe again.

Find a mirror and ask yourself, "What is the biggest thing that is holding me back from moving forward right now? What am I most afraid of?" "What is it that makes my throat close up and my chest get tight?"

You might often find that your weakness is an emotion or a message that you tell yourself in your head.

It's important to have this very clearly defined.

I recommend that you write out your weakness on a piece of paper, and go for a long walk. Write the weakness down in the past tense to help your mind understand that it is time for a transformation.

"The one thing that was holding me back from achieving my fullest potential was _____."

Meditate on the weakness. Imagine what your life will feel and look like after you have removed this weakness from your life. Clear out space in your mind for three ways in which you are going to challenge your weakness and bring it to the forefront so that you can keep marching forward.

At the end of your walk, pull the weakness out of your pocket and read it out loud. But now add this to the end of the statement…

"This obstacle is no longer a part me or who I am. I will no longer settle for a mediocre life. I will rise to the challenge and I will now live life on my own terms."

Take a moment of silence and envision your newly created lifestyle without this obstacle. Really focus on each of the senses – what will it smell like? Taste like? Sound like? Feel like? Look like?

Then grab your weakness, fold the paper up and find a way to dispose of it. Throw in the trash, slip it into a shredder, light it on fire, chuck it into the ocean. Whatever floats your boat, but you have to get rid of this weakness. You can't keep it within you.

This weakness is no longer a part of you. It is time to go out into the world and face life head on so that you can start living on purpose.

CREATING A SMART GOAL FOR YOUR MAIN CHARACTER

This isn't necessarily the rest-of-your-life goal, but this is one big over-arching accomplishment that you have wanted to do. Once you tackle one thing, it will be much easier for you to tackle anything else. After such a great accomplishment, not only is your body thriving on an endorphin kick, but psychologically, you are reprogramming the little voice in your head that spits out fear and negative talk.

Remember this step isn't about conquering the goal—this is simply to define it.

You want to create a SMART goal.

- Specific
- Measurable
- Attainable
- Relevant
- Time-bound

A Specific goal has much greater chance of being accomplished than a general goal. A specific goal will answer all of the W's: who, what, when, where and why.

A Measurable goal is one where you are keeping track of your progress and it gives incentives for you to keep going after those milestones. You know you're looking for certain quantifiable results at certain intervals.

Attainable goals are realistic and reachable. While an attainable goal may stretch a person to achieve it, the goal is not extreme.

A Relevant goal will actually meet a need or get you closer to the new big picture you are making for yourself. When you identify goals that are most important to you, you begin to figure out ways you can make them actually happen.

A Time-bound goal is intended to establish a sense of urgency and prevent goals from being overtaken by the day-to-day crises that invariably arise. Give yourself a real deadline.

If you get stuck at any point in time when you are creating this goal, consider what the one thing is that you said you were going to do but never did. Think about what you desire. What is it inside of you that you always said you were going to do, or always wanted to do, before you got busy and you forgot?

My one thing was California, and despite what some may think, it didn't require an explanation for it to make sense—I just had to go.

In August of 2014, I went on a spiritual retreat in the mountains of Boston. One day, while we were on a hike, I stopped mid-conversation and said one word to the person I was hiking with. California. She gave me a dumbfounded look and I explained that I'd always said that after I graduated college, I would get a one-way plane ticket to California.

I didn't really know why that suddenly became the issue, but sometimes intuition just takes over and tells us what we need to do. I fought it for a month or so afterwards, and then I finally gave in and booked a ticket to San Francisco. I traveled the country for an entire month, taking a full 30 days to recharge, relax from my business and give myself time to figure out what comes next.

The funny thing is, that trip was the first domino in a long maze of never-ending spirals of dominoes in my life. Each one has pushed over the next and everything just kind of fell into place.

Train Your Mind & Body

Just as an Olympic athlete may train his or her entire life to compete once in the Olympics, you will have many tasks ahead. Train properly and develop each aspect of your life in alignment with your dream lifestyle, and you will create the mindset and physical readiness for your obstacle. As Teddy Roosevelt said, believing is half the battle.

This would be a good time to get into a practice of mental and physical hardening. This doesn't mean that you have to change your attitude, as some may think. But it's time to start pushing the limits of what you are capable of and moving outside of your comfort zone.

My recommendation is two-fold: Start taking up fitness if you haven't already. Working out releases endorphins and chemicals in your brain that can push even the deepest depression away. It will be tough at first, with a lot of blood, sweat and tears. But being able to come out with a great body and a mind that has been strengthened is such a great reward.

The other recommendation is to work on yourself, whether it means working with a charity or donating your time to someone else. You must start to exercise selflessness if you want to better your mind and spirit.

I found two things to be helpful in this case. First, I found a social athletic group, and I specifically chose a sport where I didn't have to be so athletically inclined as to make sure I could avoid defeat. I joined a kickball league that played twice a week and it was a lot of fun. It got me outside of my comfort zone and made me meet new people, and you know all kinds of neat things happen when you meet new people.

I also joined a local youth group as a volunteer. I couldn't trade this experience for anything. I was in a youth group growing up and it just so happened that the same chapter that shaped me into the person I am today was in need of an advisor to watch over 15-20 high school teens. I became a big brother, in a sense, and it has been one of the most rewarding positions I've ever held.

Four years later, I'm still working with the kids multiple times a month. I think what is even more rewarding is seeing the teens that graduated my first year are now coming back from college and growing just as I am.

Strengthening your mind and your body doesn't have to come in the same shape or form in which mine did. Find your own way of strengthening. Find people who have gone through similar situations and interview them. Ask what they did while they were going through this time in their life and find out what pushed them out of their funk. I tell you my examples not to set a rule or guideline but to show how simple it is to make the change and how attainable it is.

Turning Your Enemies into Allies

We see this happen in quite a lot of super hero movies. The one person who we thought to be the bad guy gets turned around and comes over to the good side.

I think of this most when I consider bullies. A bully is more often then not someone who is hurting inside more then we are. People don't just wake up one day and decide they're going to treat someone else poorly. It's always a side effect of a certain action someone took against them or an action they took upon themselves.

Throughout your journey you'll have a lot of naysayers. You'll be ecstatic about a certain goal you want to achieve, and no matter how many times or ways you explain it to them, they will respond negatively. It's the worst feeling knowing that you spilled your guts on the table to someone that you want to support you and they turn around and try to crush your dreams.

In college a group of friends and I set out to produce a ninety-six minute long feature film on a $1,000 budget in less than twelve months. It seemed impossible, and we went to every professor in the department to try to find someone who could sign off on this as a course credit. They all laughed us away. But this was our dream and no one was going to stop us. We got to the last professor that could possibly sign off for us completing our project and just as he was about to laugh us out of his office too, something happened.

I stood up and displayed my confidence with pride. I explained that we were going to accomplish this and if we didn't, he could fail me and force me to spend another year of torture taking his classes before I graduated. We all had a moment of silence, and all I could hear in my mind was the words, *Uh-oh,* over and over again.

Here I was in my senior year of college, putting everything on the line for a dream to produce a film in honor of someone's memory. All he had to do was say yes, and, trust me, he had nothing to lose while I had everything to lose. I think this is what it means to turn your enemies into allies. When you have everything to lose and you stand up in the face of negativity and opposition, as long as you display your passion and drive, you will always prevail.

He sighed and eventually gave in, approving our project. Sure enough, less than twelve months later, in a sold-out crowd of two hundred and fifty people at a movie theater, we premiered *Six Things I Know About You,* a ninety-six-minute feature film about life, love and loss. We had stunt motorcycle drivers, donations from local businesses, props donated by the local branch of a large international corporation, most importantly, we did it.

This means two things. When you approach an enemy or someone who you think will deny support of your dream, you must stand firm. If you aren't confident in stating your mission, you won't be able to persuade others to believe that you will achieve it. The hardest part about sharing your goals with other people is that they will tell you that you can or cannot do it based on what they know to be true for them.

The other factor to keep in mind is that the person you approach might be hurting just as bad as you are, or itching to accomplish the same goal.

Perhaps consider making them see your side of the story and when they realize how much passion you have placed behind your mission, they will open up and join you.

How many times have you had a conversation that goes like this…?

You: "I really need to lose this weight; I've been eating so badly lately."

Friend: "Me too, but, you know what, it's so much easier to grab dessert from the Cheesecake Factory on the weekend."

See, your friend is already becoming an enemy because he is speaking from his point of weakness, not yours. You now have discovered that they are in the same boat as you and want to lose the weight, but they are not as mentally strong. This is a great learning and growing opportunity for you to turn someone who could have been an enemy and detrimental to your dream into a friend and partner in achieving it together. Accountability plays a huge role in ensuring that you reach success.

Taking Action – Make the Change

"The only way to make sense out of change is to plunge into it, move with it, and join the dance."

–Alan Watts

"Do you want to know who you are? Don't ask. Act! Action will delineate and define you."

–Thomas Jefferson

"Just do it."

–Nike

I always say before I'm about to approach a huge task, "There's nothing to it but to do it," and the old saying rings true. If your goal is to go skydiving, at the end of the day, the only way that happens is to jump out of the airplane. There are no other options or ways around it. Sure, you could get a similar experience in those wind tunnel places, but if your goal is jumping out of a plane, there is no alternative.

People think there is a magical secret to taking action or motivating yourself to make the change you want to see in the world.

The truth is it comes down to one thing. Grit.

How bad do you want it?

Eric Thomas, a motivational speaker said in his famous How Bad Do You Want It speech,

"Now it's time to redefine the grind. You thought it was over? Well, it's just getting started. See, this is the part. This is the part where life demands you make a life long commitment. This is the part where life demands that you make a vow, come hell or high water, that you're willing to pay the price, the full fare, where you earn your spot with effort, with sweat, with blood, with tears. And so you say, you want it as bad as you wanna breathe.

Then it's show time! It's examination time. It's time to get tested, to test your will, your endurance, it's time to test your art, to test your limits. This is the art where you re-invent yourself."

So let me ask you again, how bad do you want it? If you don't want it bad enough, then you won't take action. It's as simple as that. If your WHY is not big enough, if your purpose in making this action a reality is not the largest motivator for you, then you won't do it.

So make sure this is something you really want. Question yourself on every front, "Do I want the blood, sweat and tears that come with reaching this goal? Or will I walk away and say maybe another time and place?"

If it is important to you, you will make the time and the effort, not the excuses.

I know you were looking for a different answer, and as humans, we want the easy way out. But if there is one thing for certain, in life, there is no easy way out. There is no magic wand to wave which suddenly gives you the Disney ending. I hate to burst your bubble or ruin your parade, but your dream life happens when you happen. Nothing more and nothing less.

LIFE RE-SCRIPTED ACTION STEPS

- Find your cave and build the rope ladder to climb out. If you've read this far, you might still be stuck or lost. The only way out is up so have your bad day, then move on.

- Conquer your kryptonite by understanding half of the battle is knowing your weakness. You can't get better if you don't know your faults. Sit down for ten minutes and list out the places in your life you could improve.

- Volunteer your time and watch how your energy changes when you give to others. Find a local youth group or organization that you can assist one day a week.

- Train your mind and body whether it be in the gym or in the yoga studio. Make sure you are up and moving at all costs.

- Create three SMART goals out of your weaknesses so you can improve them over the next month. List these three goals out somewhere that you will see them every day.

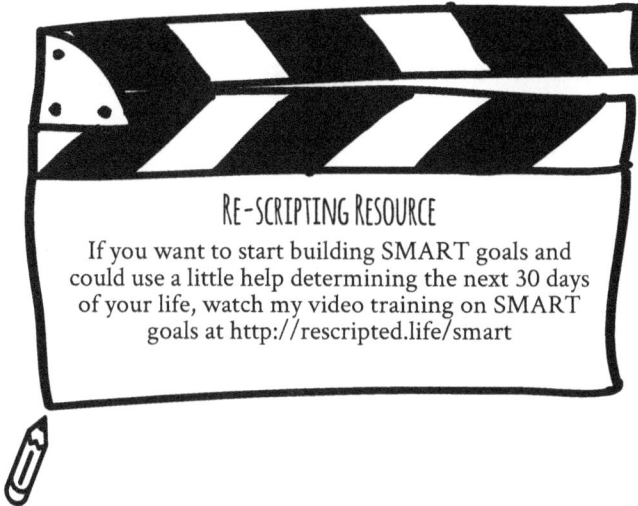

RE-SCRIPTING RESOURCE

If you want to start building SMART goals and could use a little help determining the next 30 days of your life, watch my video training on SMART goals at http://rescripted.life/smart

Act Two: The Journey of the Protagonist, Part II

"The best way to predict the future is to create it."

–Peter Drucker

We're still looking at the main character, watching the progress from the cave to the fantastic moment of achievement. Do you feel like it's getting fantastic? Or are you still confused and waiting for the parts and changes you're implementing to fall together and make sense?

Creating your dream can sometimes be confusing, but I've found if we look at the things we are avoiding the most, we'll find some hints as to where we want to go and the life we want to design.

As odd as it sounds, sometimes we get hints and clues as to where or how we will discover what it is we want to do. So when crafting your dream, keep an open mind, because you never know where the clues will come from. Some would say we're not listening well enough to our inner voice and I would agree a lot of this "dream" comes from the inside. If your dream is dictated by external factors, like what other people have or FOMO (fear of missing out), then it isn't really a dream, it's just a shiny object.

I knew that when I graduated college I had always said I'm going to walk across that stage and then get a one-way plane ticket to California. I never did it though. I was in a relationship at the time and I wanted to stay close to my significant other. I put my dream on hold and it was one of the biggest mistakes I ever made. I didn't know why California, but if you've ever had an itch to just do something with no rhyme or reason, you'll know what I'm talking about.

As it turns out, here I was four years later, buying a one-way plane ticket to San Francisco, which ultimately turned into a 30-day journey around the country. I taught myself travel hacking so I didn't have to pay much for the flights. In fact most of them were free, minus the taxes and airport fees. I used AirBnB and CouchSurfing to acquire free or cheap places to stay, and as for work? Well, let's just say I deserved a break. I had been working for a year and a half straight without a vacation, so it was overdue.

It amazed me how much I learned about myself during this time. I started to learn where I really wanted to go in life and what I wanted to do. I was crafting (from the road) and I didn't even know. I started to find things I wanted in my life as opposed to things I didn't want.

This thirty-day trip around the country actually led me to a nine-day 3,000-mile road trip with my cousin (my roommate at the time), and we traveled nearly all of the eastern United States. Upon pulling back into our driveway a little over a week later, I came up with the idea to start The Year of Purpose Podcast where I interviewed entrepreneurs and amazing people you might call "heroes" from all over the world who were living and creating a life on their own terms. This was the point where so many of the dominoes had fallen into place. My dream life was no longer a dream. It was happening.

Consider the law of attraction. The problem is we know a lot about what we don't want. The issue is we'll tend to attract more of what we don't want until we start thinking in positive terms of what we do want in our lives. It really works. You have to trust me on this one.

There are no strict guidelines to crafting your dream. In fact, I think I would be doing you a disservice if I were to just lay out a step by step plan of how to start crafting your life, because this experience will be different for everyone. The way in which I crafted my life is not exactly the best way for you to do it. However, armed with the knowledge and the proper tools, like the six disciplines you learned in the last chapter, you'll find that crafting your life is quite simple.

Find the life scripting exercise pages you finished in Chapter 7. These are the snapshots of everything that's true in your life now. If you haven't done that exercise, do it now. I urge you—DO NOT finish reading this until you've sat yourself down for an hour or two and written all of this out. There is no magic wand; there is no pill to take to fix your life. This is raw, this is real and this must happen in order for you to continue.

Did you write out your brain dump, the pages about where you are now? Good. You may continue.

LIFE RE-SCRIPTING QUESTIONS

Below I've provided some sets of questions. Answer these questions as if you are in the middle of your dream life and you are looking around and reporting on your reality. There are seven aspects of your life we'll be looking at:

- Mental and Personal Development
- Career and Business
- Financial
- Family
- Social
- Physical
- Spiritual

I highly recommend you write down your answers on paper and don't just think of the answers. You have to write this out, and I'll tell you why. Our brain knows a lot more than our mouths. The part that controls language coming out of our writing is a completely different part of the brain than the part that controls speech.

In writing this out, you are giving yourself the opportunity to see your entire script on paper. You are also now going to hold yourself accountable to this story you have created.

Anyone can type it up on the computer, close the document and just go on with their lives. I recommend getting a legal pad or a notebook that sits on your desk so you can see this script every day from here on out. I know I see mine every day.

Start below, and remember to answer these questions as if you were already in your dream life, not still in the life you just wrote out in Chapter 7.

Mental and Personal Development

- What books have I read on self-improvement in the last six months?

- How have I been clearing space in my head throughout the day to ease my mental clutter?

- Who are the people I have been surrounding myself with the most over the last two weeks?

- What are the steps I've been taking each day to become a better person?

- Am I giving my brain the stimulation it needs or am I sitting around watching TV? If I am, what can I give myself more of?

- What coaches, mentors or leaders am I following? Who should I be following?

- What is one thing I've neglected to do to take care of myself each month?

- What workshops/seminars/retreats might I be interested in participating in?

Career and Business

- What steps have I taken to advance in my job or business?

- Have I been doing a good job at networking and connecting with others?

- Do I attend networking events or social gatherings where I might meet people that can advance my status? If not, what is holding me back?

- Who are the top three people that I look up to in business or my job and why?

- What is one thing I can implement to make more money in my business or to get a promotion in my job? (Leaving your job for entrepreneurship is one option.)

- Have I asked my peers, clients or managers for feedback lately?

- What is the biggest thing that scares me in advancing in my business or job?

- What are my best qualities or experiences for the current job or business I have?

Financial

- How much is my net worth? (All savings, stocks, investments, *etc.*)

- How much am I spending each month? (Everything from coffee to rent)

- What are some things that I don't need to spend money on right now?

- What are some things I foresee myself needing to buy in the next year?

- How much am I putting away each month for retirement and savings?

- Have I met with a financial advisor or planner to go over my finances?

- Am I putting enough money away for tax season?

- How much money would I realistically like to make next year?

Family

- How often am I spending time with my family?

- Which family members do I appreciate the most and why?

- What is one thing I could improve upon that would allow me a deeper connection with my family members?

- Is there someone in my family I wish to connect with on a deeper level?

- How do my siblings and/or parents view me? Spouse/partner and/or children? What do they say are my weaknesses?

- Do I feel pressure from my family to act, live or work a certain way? If so, what is their justification?

- What is one characteristic of each of my immediate family members that I am grateful for?

- What is my role in the family and how do I affect my loved ones around me?

Social

- Who am I spending my weekends and free time with? Do I really enjoy it?

- Are there social clubs that I am a member of and would like to be more active in? If not, what groups could I look into joining?

- Which three people do I socialize with the most?

- What are my fears in meeting new people?

- What is my biggest asset or characteristic that helps me connect with new friends?

- If I died today, what would my friends say about me at my funeral?

- What bad habits do my friends have that I should avoid?

- How can I get more active in the community to meet more people that will support my dream lifestyle?

Physical

- How many times a week am I active and what am I doing?

- What are the biggest changes I'd like to see with my body image and composition?

- What are the phrases and words I tell myself when I look at myself in the mirror?

- What sports or activities would I be interested in trying out?

- Am I walking at least 10,000 steps a day or do I sit mostly at the computer? How can I change that?

- What injuries should I be aware of when it comes to my body movement?

- What are some ways I could be more active throughout my day?

- Why am I not comfortable in my own body as it is?

Spiritual

- Have I been active in my faith and religion? If not, how would I like to change that? (Perhaps you don't follow one, and that's OK too!)

- Am I taking time to meditate or time for silence throughout my day?

- What does my energy level feel like when I wake up in the morning?

- What does my energy level feel like when I go to bed? What troubles do I have falling asleep?

- What is one thing I could do to get in touch with my inner spirit more often?

- Have I really sat down and affirmed my beliefs in how I should live life?

- Am I living my life on my own terms or do I base my principles off of what others have taught me to be their limiting beliefs?

- Does my spirit feel at ease with where I am in life or is it time for a change?

You've discovered the entire process a hero must take to rise to the top from climbing out of the cave to understanding your kryptonite and creating a goal for your main character. Next, it's time to train your mind and body and turn your enemies into allies. After that, you'll take action and craft your dream. It's a long process and that's exactly why I decided to provide you with thought-provoking questions that will get you better answers.

Now that we've covered the path you'll be experiencing in the very near future, I think it's time for a break, a bathroom break that is!

We all know that movies are long and if you stopped at the concession stand, that super-sized Super Freezee has more than likely made its way through your system. It's time to take a step out for just a moment.

Life Re-Scripted Action Steps

- Utilize the law of attraction and catch yourself in the act of being negative. Write down your negative thoughts or feelings on notes that you can throw into a negativity jar – keep the negativity out of your life. Accept what is and keep going.
- Complete the previous life re-scripting questions in this chapter.
- Write a meter from zero to ten and rate yourself in each of the seven aspects of life mentioned above. Zero would mean you are doing the least to improve while ten would mean you are an expert. Ask yourself why you rated yourself in certain areas that score lower. List out three action steps for each aspect of your life.

Re-scripting Resource
If you want to know where you stand on a spectrum in each of the seven main categories of your life, watch my video training on the seven foundations of life at
http://rescripted.life/spectrum

The Bathroom Break

"If you want a happy ending, that depends, of course, on where you stop your story."

–Orson Welles

Chapter nine covered quite possibly the most important part of your journey: you received the roadmap of what is about to happen next for you. I don't think anyone ever gave me hints as to what to expect in life, so I can only be jealous of how fortunate of a place you are in right now.

I can tell you this because, having experienced all of these places in life from finding my kryptonite to crafting my dream, I have lived it. I was also surprised when I found out that our beloved super heroes in the movies tend to follow almost the same path as we do.

But if you've ever considered taking a break from life, that's what this chapter is all about—what do you do when you are stepping out for a bit and you run into FOMO?

FOMO, or Fear Of Missing Out, is a common occurrence with moviegoers and life attendees alike. You want to be sure you never step out when it's just getting to the good part.

Inevitably, when you are watching a movie, if you've choked down a pan of nachos and a large Super Freezee, you're going to have to pee.

You have this moment where you weigh the pros and cons. You could slip out now for that badly needed relief and maybe miss something, or you could sit and wriggle in acute discomfort, not leaving but really, really distracted and hoping you make it without exploding.

When I was a year and a half into my business, I found myself waking up for the longest time thinking, *I don't want to be here anymore.* Part of it was the physical location of being in the same town where I'd lived my entire life, and the other part was mental. I was overworked, burnt out, and exhausted of life and everything involved with it. After breaking off a two-year relationship and realizing that some changes needed to be made, I signed up for a four day spiritual retreat.

I had never tried anything like this before and honestly had no idea what to expect. But with yoga on a dock of a private lake and organic meals in the woods of the Berkshires (Boston), you really can't go wrong. We did everything from group trust work with a high ropes course to channeling our inner fears around a bonfire. It was a magical weekend that I'll never forget for the rest of my life. But there was one moment that always sticks out to me as the turning point.

We were hiking up a mountain one afternoon and mid conversation I turned to the person I was talking to and just said, "I have to go to California. I don't know why but I need to go."

Sometimes taking a break from life leads to the greatest discoveries and transformations. We're scared to do it because we might have families, significant others, and obligations that we believe hold us back. But I don't think I would have ever landed where I am now had it not been for that break (and a few others that I took).

The trip to California, which I took two months later, actually turned into a month of travel-hacking and couch-surfing around the country. I took an entire month off from my business, my family and my life to find out who I was with all the external factors stripped away. No one I knew really understood why I did it, but I knew deep down that it was the right thing to do.

When you get down to the very core of who you are, that's when you really get the opportunity to rebuild. Now I know this whole process won't happen while you take a ninety second bathroom break but I can tell you, a month hiatus from life feels like a quick break in the grand scheme of things.

That month of travel lead to a nine-day, 3,000 mile road trip in December, which lead to starting my podcast, The Year of Purpose Podcast in January of 2015, which brings me to a promise.

When I got back home from that road trip, I realized that there are two types of people on this planet. There are those who set New Year's resolutions and stick to them, and those who give up two weeks into the year. I didn't want to be the latter. So I promised myself 2015 was going to be my best year yet. It wasn't enough to set three or four goals because, the truth is, I should be striving every day, every moment, to make the most out of what I have and to experience all life has to offer.

You only get one chance to live life and if you do it right, you won't want another.

Stepping away from everything allowed me to cut out the B.S. and get down to the foundation. I got to find out what I do when I'm away from home for a long period of time. I learned what it's like to traverse a new city. I found out what it's like to share a small and unfamiliar apartment with a new female friend who randomly decided to travel with me. I found out who the real Zephan is. You can do this too.

Maybe your bathroom break only takes three minutes and that's ok, but whatever break you take, be sure to make the most out of it. You could hold it in and face the consequences of not being present, hoping you make it without exploding for the rest of your story. Or you could take a risk by running to the bathroom for a couple minutes. The only downside is you could potentially miss a good part. But the rest of the movie is on the other side of that break, and the only way to finish out the story is by jumping back in and enjoying the ride.

The bathroom break, or the hiatus from life, as I call it, was the result of the epiphany I had on top of the mountain. Some might think they can't create this moment as easily as I did. Trying to make this happen at any given time is like asking a magician to pull a rabbit out of his ear while he's naked in the shower. He can't just make something out of nothing: he doesn't have his tools with him and he certainly isn't prepared for this.

One movie that reminds me of how you can generate this moment for yourself is *I, Robot.* The movie is based in a future world where robots have become servants to the humans and a big conglomerate is creating and selling these things like hot cakes. Everyone and their grandmother has a robot to cook, wash the dishes, do the chores, *etc.* But Will Smith plays good old-fashioned police Detective Spooner, and he hasn't quite bought into the hype.

One day he discovers that his friend, Dr. Alfred Lanning (played by James Cromwell), who is the inventor of the laws that govern these robots (Not harming people, and all that) was found dead on the mezzanine of his office building after seemingly throwing himself from a balcony many floors above. I get it; it's dark and depressing, but hang tight with me for a second.

Our hero, Detective Spooner, shows up to investigate, and finds that Dr. Lanning left behind a hologram that can answer only very limited questions. Spooner wants to know why Dr. Lanning killed himself, but the hologram doctor simply replies that his responses are limited and he cannot answer that.

So Spooner, getting creative with his questions, takes into consideration the possibility that a robot had something to do with it and asks if the reason the doctor is dead is because there is an issue with the laws that govern these robots. Ultimately Lanning's hologram replies, "That, Detective, is the right question."

So what does this all have to do with creating a space in time where you have enough clarity to figure out your next big step in life? It has everything to do with it! It's all about asking the right questions. You see, we are our own worst enemies. In a sense, we're much like Dr. Lanning's hologram in that we have very limited responses programmed in. When we're searching for answers for the hard questions such as, "What is my purpose in life?" or "How will I ever become successful?" we usually can't come up with a good response.

We're similar to these robots that have been programmed with laws that dictate how they should function because we've been living a certain story, a certain script. It isn't until you can find the right question that you'll find the right answer.

I couldn't just walk up that same mountain and ask myself what I should do with my life. The big thing I needed to tell myself was, "Hey, remember that thing you said you were going to do before you got all busy and you forgot? You should really go do that thing."

This was how I came up with going to California. I remembered that when I'd been getting ready to graduate college, I'd planned on getting a one way plane ticket to Los Angeles, where I would find my way into the video industry because that was what I wanted more than anything at that time.

The truth was, I could do video work from anywhere, it wasn't necessarily that I had to go to LA for the profession, but I had to go because my intuition was telling me there was something more to it.

So I finally, after much deliberation, went to California. It only took me five years to get there but I did it, and the surprising thing was everything fell into place.

You see, you could sit there in the movie of your life, bouncing your foot up and down having to pee all you want. You can deliberate on whether or not you'll miss something good and you can wrestle with the FOMO. But you could make the decision to get up and take the hiatus from where you are right now.

You can make the decision to listen to what you said you were going to do all those years ago, because chances are, that was your true path and you decided to keep watching the movie instead. Your bladder hasn't been emptied so that need to go do that thing is still there. You just have to get back to your roots to find out what that thing is.

So ask yourself what it is you always said you wanted to do? Chances are, that is the one thing you should do right now, regardless of the what-ifs that will instantly take over your brain when you begin to consider it.

This is the part of your story where you start asking better questions. Jump out for your pee break, and then come back and hang on.

It's all different from here on out, and different can be exciting, scary, frustrating and exhilarating all at once.

Life Re-Scripted Action Steps

- Take a day to care for yourself. Getting caught up in self-improvement is great but if you don't pamper yourself, it's hard to keep going. Head over to a local massage therapist or spa for the day and take a load off.

- Replace your regrets with your dreams. Whenever you start thinking about what you should have done, shift your focus to the changes you are making in your life now. It requires far less energy to stay positive.

- Teach yourself deep breathing strategies that you can deploy to give yourself a break during work. Sixty seconds is all it takes.

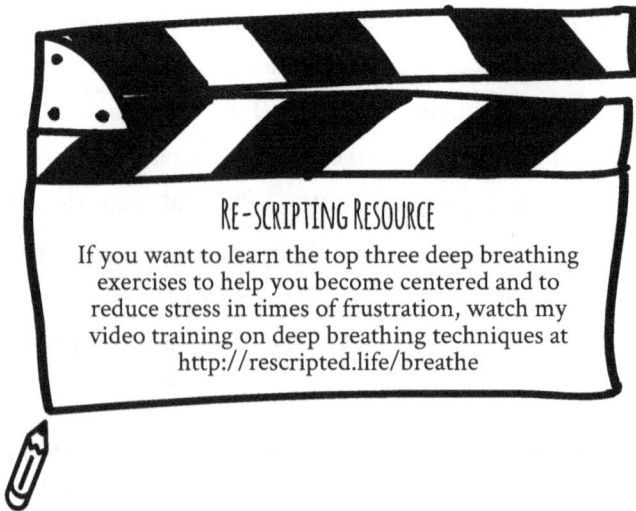

Re-Scripting Resource
If you want to learn the top three deep breathing exercises to help you become centered and to reduce stress in times of frustration, watch my video training on deep breathing techniques at http://rescripted.life/breathe

Act Three: The Plot Twist

"He who can no longer pause to wonder and stand rapt in awe, is as good as dead; his eyes are closed."

–Albert Einstein

Sometimes taking a break and stepping back to ask better questions is all you need to transform your life. I know that for me, if I had simply known how to ask better questions, nothing else in this book would have mattered because it would have all come naturally. But of course, it's only right that I provide you with the best tools for designing life on your own terms.

So you stepped out to take a quick pee break and you're back. It took a little bit to find your seat because of the dim light in the theater and the path wasn't quite clear. Now you're trying to get your bearings as you settle back into the movie. Then it hits you... You took a break and missed parts of the story. Now you don't know how what's happening now fits with what was going on when you left.

The bathroom break didn't exactly fix things. Just like taking a moment away from your life doesn't quite fix it.

Running away from problems doesn't fix anything. I think back to when I was diagnosed as a teenager with bipolar manic-depressive disorder and a panic and anxiety disorder. Drowning me in medication didn't make it go away. It just numbed me to my problems. Ultimately, it was something deep inside that I had to work out and work through, and the medicine enabled me to do so.

Just like your break from life is simply a band aid that makes the desperation inside let up, you have to take what you learned during the change and calm that the bandaid brings and apply it to your life now.

When you have a panic disorder, your anxiety can attack at any moment. It can be truly debilitating and you might be convinced your life is ending. It's quite hard to think objectively when you are hyperventilating. But for me, taking the medicines that have a calming effect allowed me to reason with myself and understand that there was nothing physically going on in my body, such as closing off my throat. All of it was in my head.

So how do you really determine your purpose in life and jump back into your story after you've taken a step back to see the whole picture?

Allow me to introduce the plot twist. This is where things are going to change for you and your story is going to dramatically alter forever.

The Circle of Purpose

You've seen the graphic that shows a big circle and inside the circle is the label "Comfort zone" and then all the way outside the circle are the words, "Where the magic happens." People will try to tell you that you find your purpose when you step out of your comfort zone. While this is somewhat true, it also is not the whole picture. It goes back to asking the right questions and leaves you at square one with figuring out what to do with your life.

Far too many people are searching for purpose in the wrong place. They think, *Oh, if I just do this one thing,* or *Oh, when I finally get to this next step...* and they never get there. What is it about finding your purpose that is so unbelievably hard? Alan Watts, a famous philosopher said this:

"When we finally got down to something, which the individual says he really wants to do, I will say to him, you do that and forget the money, because, if you say that getting the money is the most important thing, you will spend your life completely wasting your time. You'll be doing things you don't like doing in order to go on living, that is to go on doing things you don't like doing, which is stupid. Better to have a short life that is full of what you like doing than a long life spent in a miserable way.

And after all, if you do really like what you're doing, it doesn't matter what it is, you can eventually turn it—you could eventually become a master of it. It's the only way to become a master of something, to be really with it. And then you'll be able to get a good fee for whatever it is. So don't worry too much."

It starts with asking better questions, and you've already done that if you went through the process of writing out your script of where you are now in act one and act two. If you haven't done that already, you might want to go back to do that. And when I say might, I mean don't continue reading this book until you have done so.

Your purpose is going to be discovered at the intersection of four things. These four things are: something that the world needs, something that you love, something that you are great at, and something that you can get paid for. If you have something that you love and the world needs it, then it is a mission, which is great, but if you aren't great at it or you aren't getting paid, it's not going to be very satisfying. If you are really good at a certain task, and you love it, you might think that it is your purpose in life and you would be pretty close, but at this point, it's still just a passion because it isn't making a lasting impact on the world.

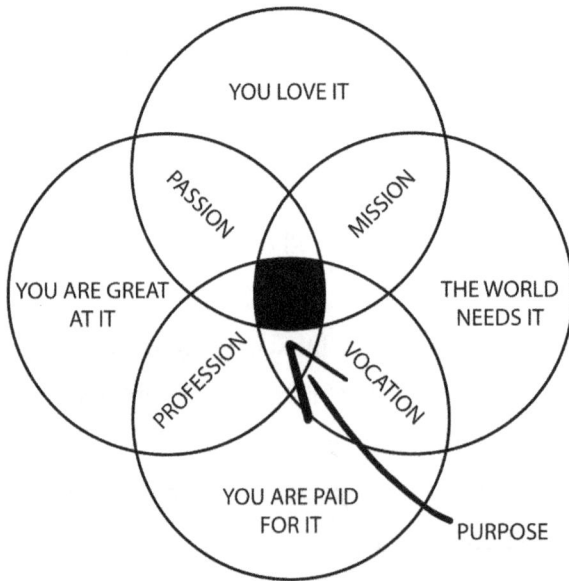

When you give to others and share your gift with the world, your purpose will start to clearly define itself. So now let's take the example of getting paid for something. I used to get paid to fix broken phones (something which the world sure needs), and I was great at it, too! But I didn't love getting yelled at by angry customers all the time and I certainly didn't love working for someone else's agenda. It was a vocation, and once I became really good at it, I might as well have considered it my profession.

So if we should be doing something that the world needs, clearly that has to be our purpose, right? Well, not exactly. You can love what you are doing and as long as the world needs more of it, you have a great mission and a great story to tell, but there are two missing factors. You need to get paid (after all you have expenses), and you have to be great at it. Otherwise you may find yourself discouraged later down the road.

So a quick exercise in finding your purpose is below:

Grab a pen or a pencil (once again, no computers allowed), and start writing things down in four columns on a piece of paper. Column one is what you are great at, number two is what you love, number three what you can get paid for, and number four is something that the world needs. Set ten minutes on the timer and work your way down one column. Then repeat for ten minutes for the second column, and so on. If you get stuck, stay in that column and start asking yourself "Why." Why are you good at a certain thing or why you love what you wrote down. Pencil in a quick note as to why you picked those answers. After forty minutes you should have at least twenty items in each column.

Start circling items and connecting them to items that fall under different columns, noting where they align. For example, I am really good at filmmaking because I am a good storyteller so my one thing I'm really good at is telling stories. I absolutely love being able to experience the stories of others by growing and learning from their lessons. The world needs a lot more people like me who want to live a meaningful life because if we aren't living on purpose, why else are we here? Lastly, and this was the tricky part, getting paid for what you love, what you are good at and what the world needs more of.

This is often where people get stuck—the whole money thing. The Internet is a powerful tool, in this case, with the capability of connecting people thousands of miles apart. We are in a day and age where money can be made easily. Whether you are teaching someone else, sharing your message with someone else or creating a service/ product that makes an task easier for someone else, it is totally possible to profit from the things you love all while making a difference in the lives of those who need it.

At the end of the day, your purpose isn't going to come from a quote, or a diagram, or even a motivational poster. Your purpose is already inside of you. You have each of these things already: a desire to make a difference in the world, something you are good at, something you are passionate about and something that makes you money. While they might not intersect just yet, there is a connection. If you did the exercise, you'll find that it's pretty easy to figure out the gift you want to give to the world.

I challenge you to find a new and creative way to change the world with the knowledge you have just been given. In fact, I dare you to go out and set the world on fire (metaphorically, speaking of course), because we need more people like you to pave the path for others. While you might feel a bit lost right now, I can assure you, the very fact that you have picked up this book shows that you have the drive and ambition to make every day special.

So our main acts are coming to the end. In Act One we talked about the 5X Life Hack Rule also known as the Struggle to Hustle Golden Ratio: A little bit of STRUGGLE combined with the right amount of HUSTLE are the only two ingredients in EDITING your story, that lead to a LIFE that you LOVE.

You can remember the 5XLHR by simply just reciting the word, SHELL. In Act Two, I taught you exactly what you can expect from the journey of the protagonist or, in a sense, your future story. This is not only based on what has happened in my life and so many others' lives, but the core of this is derived from the chronology of a hero rising to greatness.

There's a reason why we're so attracted to comic books-turned-movies like *Iron Man* or *The Dark Knight*. It's because they are just embellished versions of our own lives, real people with weaknesses, love interests, obstacles and pain just like us. Then lastly, we just reviewed the plot twist, where you can truly determine what your purpose is in less than an hour all while asking yourself better questions and gaining clarity on what to do next.

But it's not over... yet.

Life Re-Scripted Action Steps

- Check in with yourself again. We've covered a lot of pieces of your script and the overwhelm may be setting in. Let's combat this with some positive self talk.

- Ask better questions when you start to get stuck. Instead of asking what the world can give to you, start asking what you can gift to the world.

- Pick something that you really love and keep it to yourself. There might be something that you love to do, but you aren't the best at it and you can't really make money with it. It's always nice to keep something to yourself as a hobby.

- Complete the circle of purpose activity mentioned previously. You might be surprised what you discover about your purpose in life.

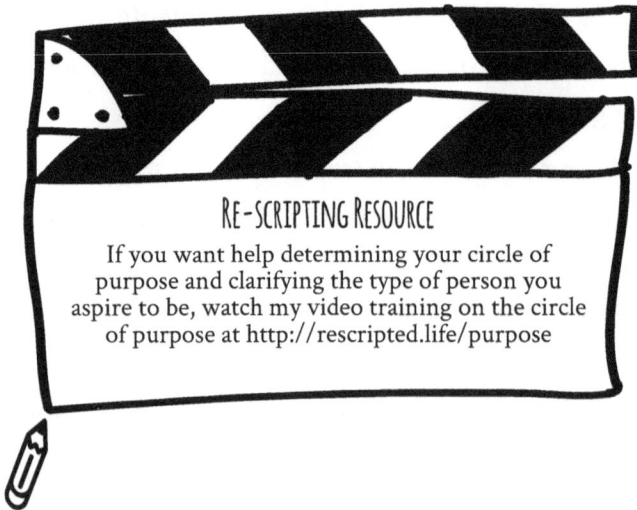

Re-Scripting Resource

If you want help determining your circle of purpose and clarifying the type of person you aspire to be, watch my video training on the circle of purpose at http://rescripted.life/purpose

And They Lived ___ Ever After

"I write the last line, and then I write the line before that. I find myself writing backwards for a while, until I have a solid sense of how that ending sounds and feels. You have to know what your voice sounds like at the end of the story, because it tells you how to sound when you begin."

– John Irving

We all want to have that Disney ending with our lives, but why stop there? Why does the ending have to be at the end of our lives? You see, when a movie ends and the guy gets the princess and goes off into the sunset, the story doesn't stop there. The movie might be over at this point, and from a story plot standpoint, this is a perfect way to close the curtains. But life doesn't end just because we have reached a point of success.

The show must go on for us.

Our stories are constantly evolving, and even if you took the 5XLHR, or the hiatus, and implemented them, there is still work to be done.

You get many chances in your life to make a sequel for your story, and it doesn't have to stop here. I'm sure that after applying the lessons you've learned in this book, you'll want to take your life to new heights again. I think of my life much like the Lord of the Rings series. There are tons of thick, word-rich stories that make up the larger, overarching theme. At one point in time, I'll be lost in the woods on my quest for what seems like years, but in the end, I'll always face my demons, come out on top, and find my way back home.

So I wanted to share with you the story of someone I define as a true hero, someone who re-scripted his life to make a difference in the world, to get paid for making that difference, and he loved every second of it because he was good at it. His name was Lenny B. Robinson, and he was known as the Baltimore Batman.

Lenny grew up in Baltimore, Maryland, running a highly successful business that he later sold for a large sum of money. His first installment of the story might have ended there, but he chose to explore a new journey. He could have become a millionaire and just lived out his days on a yacht. I can see how one might enjoy the peace and serenity but, Lenny made a new story.

Lenny was an American superhero who dressed up in a full Batman costume. His rise to fame happened in 2012, when he was pulled over by a police officer for a license plate issue on his Bat-mobile. The video went viral, and instead of settling for a few moments of fame, he decided to do something about it, something that the world needed more of.

He set out on a mission "to entertain ill and terminally ill children by appearing to them as Batman and teaching them that just as Batman fights battles, no matter how hard or long their health battles may be, with strength of will and determination, there is always hope!" He visited sick children in hospitals, handed out Batman gear to kids who were battling cancer and other diseases, and signed autographs.

On August 16, 2015, Lenny's story tragically came to an end. He was coming home from a visit at a hospital with his Bat-mobile, when it suddenly broke down on the side of the road. He was struck by a Toyota Camry and pronounced dead at the scene. His burial was attended by hundreds of those whose lives he had impacted. They even covered his casket with the Batman logo.

While the community grieved, I drove by one of the local delis to find a giant inflated Batman figurine balloon that was tied down kneeling up on a hill and saluting the road. Lenny's purpose in life was certainly fulfilled. He found a way to love, to master, to profit and to give the world something that it needed so much more of.

Disney endings are unrealistic. We don't literally get carried away on horseback or live in a beautiful castle. The only thing that doesn't work in this metaphor is all those silly endings. Life isn't tied up in a nice bow like a Cinderella story. Life is always a series of failures and successes, and never in any particular order. But it's all about what you make of those failures and successes, and I know that there will be heroes like Lenny who will rise up from nothing and make a difference in the world.

When I think of my legacy and what I want to leave behind as the curtains close, I don't think about the number of people I want at my funeral, nor do I imagine how my life would be celebrated, because I have no control over that. But I do have control over how I make people feel and how they remember the emotions that I was able to pull out of them—the best of them and the worst.

So place an ending on this chapter of your life, this chapter that isn't fulfilling your needs and desires. It's time to re-write the script and live out your dreams.

The movie is coming to a close and we have to give it a proper sendoff. As with any movie, the screen will fade to black, music will start playing and the credits will roll. But for now, it's time to celebrate you and your journey through this movie. Welcome to your life, re-scripted.

LIFE RE-SCRIPTED ACTION STEPS

- Create a legacy statement, use powerful words that reflect the way in which you would like your life to be remembered.
- Ask your friends what they would remember you for. People remember how you made them feel, not what you did for them. Find out what emotions you are best at bringing out of others.
- Write a manifesto that inspires and empowers you to fulfill your dreams and truly design a life on your own terms. Frame it on your wall as a reminder that YOU are possible.

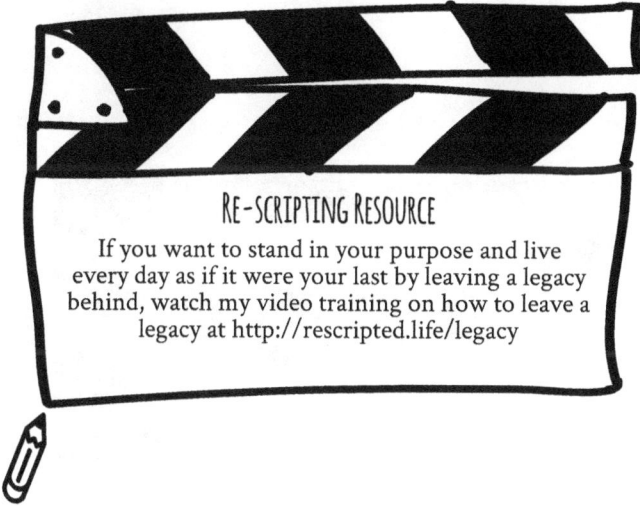

Re-scripting Resource

If you want to stand in your purpose and live
every day as if it were your last by leaving a legacy
behind, watch my video training on how to leave a
legacy at http://rescripted.life/legacy

Closing Credits

"I went to the woods because I wished to live deliberately, to front only the essential facts of life, and see if I could not learn what it had to teach, and not, when I came to die, discover that I had not lived."

-Henry David Thoreau

The movie is coming to the end, the music is slowly fading out and the screen goes to black. The curtains haven't closed quite yet because there is still one more thing left to do. Some folks say that the most important part of the movie is the main character overcoming their struggle. But I say it's the ability to thank everyone, down to the most seemingly insignificant of contributions. Each one of those people who played a role in making sure this story happened.

On a feature film set, you might have hundreds of people to credit, from the lighting designers and sound developers to the makeup artists and stunt doubles. When I worked on set for season three of *House of Cards*, the famous Kevin Spacey TV show on Netflix, I observed chefs, first aid medics, and even a man who had the sole job of changing signs and names on doors. As we were filming inside of an office building, he was tasked with the job of masking over the current nameplate on the offices and creating a new one on the spot. You can bet that guy was credited at the end of the show.

Look at where you are right now. Not your physical surroundings, but rather the successes and the failures that have occurred in your life. Every family member, friend, mentor, bully, enemy and sandwich maker involved in your life was placed there for a reason. We might not know the how and why, but every single thing that has happened has gotten us to this exact moment.

Take a moment to be thankful. Feel the gratitude that comes out of knowing even the worst people in your life, the ones that have harmed you or done wrong by you, are the reason you are able to read this book right now and make a change for the life of your dreams.

I'm thankful for the negative people that have entered my life. Each person that I've had to turn around and say, "Just watch me" to has been a stepping stone into my greatness. I hope you'll see those as a blessing in disguise in your life as well.

Many people who have experienced near-death moments talk about flashing lights or seeing the people in their life fly by like a movie on a screen. It's funny how we as humans associate the chronological process of a film with the story of our lives. At the end of the movies, hundreds of names fly up the screen as quick as a single blip on the radar and just as quickly gone. Each name was a small nudge in our existence to put us on the path we end up taking.

We should be so fortunate as to be a blip on someone else's credits. As mentioned before, it's not about what you do for yourself, but your purpose comes from discovering what gift you are going to gift to the world.

I challenge you to look at all the people in your life and consider those who haven't entered your life yet. Find out what gifts you have that you can use to have a greater impact for them. My alma mater, James Madison University, had a slogan to "Make Your Mark on Madison." What is the mark you want to leave on someone else's story? Will you be a supporting actor or "store clerk #2?" How will you spend your time in that role?

Throughout you life you're going to be creating new stories and ending old ones. One of my favorite authors, J.K. Rowling, said, "There's always room for a story that can transport people to another place." I agree with her sentiment; there is always space for another story, one of growth, enlightenment, empowerment, development, or even physical transportation. Somehow deep inside, part of you knows what this story is. The only way for you to pull this story out is to step into your greatness and keep faith. Remember that somewhere, further down the road, your story will leave someone else remembering how they felt because they were a part of it. That, my friends, is how to lead a life of purpose, a life re-scripted.

So consider this...

At the end of your life, the movie fades to black, the music chimes in and the credits start to roll. What's the song that is playing right now? Is this song indicative of how you lived your life or is it more of a song that you *wish* represented your life?

Did you earn this song? Did you work for each and every word in the lyrics? Maybe it's instrumental, but perhaps the emotion behind it truly dictates the person you want to be. It's time to start earning that song. Making sure that every day when you wake up, the song that plays in the credits of your life is the theme song accompanying each new day.

Life Re-Scripted Action Steps

- Find the song that plays in the credits of your life. Listen to it over and over while visualizing what your life will be like when you implement the changes you've discovered in this book.
- Go back through the action steps in this book and create a calendar. Start setting goal dates of when you will complete each task and set reminders on your phone or computer so you don't skip a day. Simply using an additional ten minutes of your day to make these changes is the best way to start.
- Thank everyone that has been a part of your life so far. The heroes, the villains, and even the guy who ran out and bought you coffee.

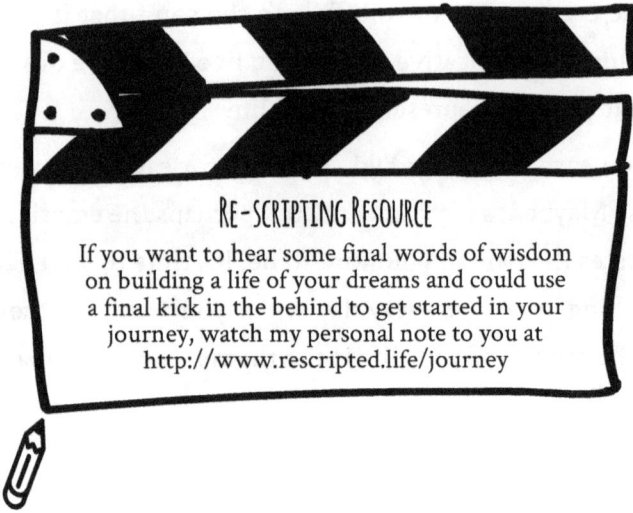

Re-scripting Resource

If you want to hear some final words of wisdom on building a life of your dreams and could use a final kick in the behind to get started in your journey, watch my personal note to you at http://www.rescripted.life/journey

Post Credits Scene

"That's the thing about leaks: sometimes they aren't misinterpreted or false. They're real story elements that the filmmakers were hoping to introduce to the audience in a darkened movie theater."

–Colin Trevorrow

Some of my favorite movies leak a hint as to what might come in the next movie, whether it be the next evil villain or sometimes just a funny gag to finish off the story. I think that quite possibly the best way to finish off this one is to talk about the one thing that is holding you back from truly living a life re-scripted.

So, what I hope that you leave with from this chapter is basically a sense of where you are in life. So what fears do you have? What obstacles are you trying to overcome? Is it in life, in work—anywhere in your life?

So, on top of public speaking, there are two big fears that I really grew up with. The first one is roller coasters, and the second one is needles.

When I was about fourteen or fifteen, I was on this sporting team that traveled all across the country. In the summers, we would go to competitions. And one day we had some time off, so we went to a theme park. I said to my coach—being fourteen or fifteen and thinking I'm invincible—"We're going on a roller coaster before I leave today. Make sure that I go on a roller coaster!"

That was a bad idea. I instantly regretted telling her that, because I knew that she would make sure I did not leave the park that day without going on a roller coaster. And I had never been on a roller coaster, so I had no clue what to expect.

So we got into the park and she grabbed a map of the rides, and found the biggest, baddest roller coaster. Little did I know, it was actually the third largest drop on a roller coaster in the country. And she said "Let's go!" and I go, "Uh oh..." But we went over, we got in line. I started to get nervous. Really nervous. More nervous than speaking in front of a crowd of people. Coach said, "What?" and I said, "I'm nervous!"

Coach replied, "I've got heart problems, I've got high blood pressure, I'm on seven medications, and you can't get on the ride?" Then I was like, "Oh, okay. Man, you really have it that bad? I guess I'm doing okay here. Let's do this." So I got up into the seat, and we got buckled in and we went up the big climb to the top.

And right before we got to the top, she turned and said to me, "You know all that stuff I said to you while we were waiting in line?" And she didn't say "stuff," she used a different word, but you can guess that one – remember where chicken salad comes from? At this point, I had a death grip on the seat on front of me. And I internally freaked out, and she said, "I lied!"

The whole way down, I screamed, "I-i-i-i-i-i'm-m-m-m-m gon-n-n-n-n-na ki-i-i-il-l-l-l yo-o-o-o-o-u-u!"

And, from that day on, I've been afraid of roller coasters. Why? Because I had a bad experience. I always associated roller coasters with being lied to. That's what I remember that as.

The other fear I have is needles. When I was growing up, my parents chose not to vaccinate me. Now we can talk about that issue another time, but the point is, I did not have many experiences with needles in my arm. And so, going into that, when I was probably fifteen or sixteen, I had to go in for just a typical blood test.

I sat down, and the guy wrapped the stretchy thing around my arm, and he pulled out the tubes one by one, really slowly, and next thing I know, there was eleven...twelve...thirteen tubes on the table. I was just thinking, *I don't know if there is enough blood in my body to fill all these tubes.* And I passed out.

He hadn't even pulled the needle out of the drawer yet, and I passed out. And that fear was because I had this idea that when he stuck this needle into my arm, either A) I was going to deflate like a balloon and just pop, or B) it was going to hurt so bad that I was going to pass out anyway! But before we even got to the needle, I was gone.

There's a difference between these two fears. One of them was based off of this preconceived idea of what was going to happen. Because I had never experienced it before, but I had this idea of what was going to happen, I passed out from the needle. Versus the experience with the roller coaster. I had been lied to. So it was actually a bad experience.

So fears are because either it is a bad experience, or because you *think* it's going to be a bad experience.

So how do you overcome that? How do you take an obstacle like fear that you have in your life, where you're stuck, and get past that? Well, it's really hard, to be honest. You know, Nike says, "Just do it." It's not very easy. But if you can understand that it's something as simple as a potentially false notion in your mind of what it's going to be like, you can start from there and bring it down to the basics and break it down to what really is going to happen.

If you go in for a blood test, the best thing that could happen is they come back and say you're totally healthy. Wouldn't you want to know that? You would. So if you focus on the positive, you can overcome this preconceived notion in your mind that the needle will be awful.

Now, with the other event, with having a bad experience...it happened already, right? You can't go back and just erase it. But the way the mind works is that you can generate a new experience that overrides the emotions from the past.

What are you afraid of? Drowning? Snakes? Anything else? Are you afraid to even tell someone what your fear is? So everyone has fear, right? Whether you're afraid of clowns, whether you're afraid of not making enough money in your business and not supporting your family, when you create a more positive scenario in your mind it kind of wipes out the preconceived notion in your mind.

So how do you do this? Well, maybe you decide "I'll buy tickets to go to the circus! But I'm going to have a couple of drinks beforehand, we'll laugh it up, and it's going to be a really good time." And from that point, you realize that clowns are just people acting in costumes, right? It's not as big of a deal anymore.

I'm not asking you to go and be a snake wrangler for a day. That's probably not the best way to go about it if you fear something that really is potentially dangerous. But when you can, create an experience that will give you a good memory about that event. It's going to be much better off for you in the long run.

So what did I do with this knowledge once I figured it out?

I was only about fifteen when I figured out these two things. When I graduated college, I had a job just two weeks after I walked across the stage. I thought I was set for the rest of my life, but a year after working there, I showed up to work one day, a lawyer walked in and handed me a pink slip. "You just lost your job. The company got bought out. We're moving to Chicago. Everyone is let go." And I got crushed.

I was afraid of doing something great at that point in time, because I thought that if I just went out and got a job, it would most likely just end in failure again. Or it would be a huge disappointment. So I settled and I went on unemployment.

For a good three months, I freelanced while I was on unemployment. I learned how to get my own clients and I talked to some people from my past company and I said "Hey, look, the company got sold. I need some work. You know that I do great video work there. I'd love to come do some work for you." And fortunately, three or four people actually did step up and contract with me.

A little while later, I actually got hired to work at the Apple Store Genius Bar. Remember way back in the first chapter I told you about the awful day that was the end for me? Remember that former client who watched me tune out and challenged me on a bar napkin?

Here's how he got me to break past my fear of another job disaster.

When he got that little napkin, he pulled out a pen and he said, "How much do you make right now?" I was really embarrassed, but I told him, "I make thirty thousand dollars a year. I still live in my parents' house." So he wrote $30,000 at the top, and he wrote $0 on the bottom.

Then he drew twelve little steps on it, and he said "Pull out your phone. Open up your calculator. Take thirty thousand and divide it by two hundred and fifty." (This was to account for working five days a week for fifty weeks out of the year, assuming I took off for two). The math ultimately came down to one hundred and twenty dollars per day. He said "That is what you have to make to replace this job." Now I could go out and mow four or five lawns for a $120, right?

I didn't want to, but the point was that it was that simple to replace that amount of money. He broke it down into a goal that I could believably and easily achieve. I was no longer facing the huge fear of trying to replace $30,000. I was looking at replacing $120, five times a week.

Well, the next day I walked into work with a resignation letter. Two weeks later, I started my business ZMBmedia, a Baltimore based video production company. And it was a huge learning curve—networking, doing everything right, researching online…and I kept running into these obstacles. I had to pay for an accountant, a lawyer, I had to set up an LLC. It is not easy when you're a broke kid without a job trying to start a business.

But I overcame each and every fear by saying, "Well, let's break this down into smaller steps. How can I go about making this happen? Well, I need an LLC. Who gives you an LLC? A lawyer sets up your LLC. Okay, let's ask around. Does anyone know a lawyer that'll get me an LLC?" And an LLC got formed.

So it was no longer "I need to start a business." Now it was these smaller, easier, completely doable steps. That has gotten me to where I am now. So I think it's really important to realize that whatever the fear is—whether it's a bad experience or this bad idea in your mind of what it could be like—as long as you find a way to make it positive and break it down into those smaller steps, you're going to be able to overcome that.

The same thing happened again. I was a year and a half into my business and said "What do I really want to do?" Well, I'd worked for a year and a half, and I wanted to travel for a whole month. I wanted to leave on November 1st and I didn't want to come back until the 30th." And I did it.

I was afraid. I had never traveled alone. But I taught myself how to travel hack so the flights cost me next to nothing. I was turned on to Airbnb and CouchSurfing. I also realized with the power of social media you can usually find friends pretty much anywhere who have an extra sofa.

And so from November 1st, I left, and the first step was this: buy a plane ticket. I didn't view it as "I'm gonna be gone for a whole month." Because if I looked at it that way, the fear came up. "Well, I'm not working for a whole month. Where does the money come from?

What happens when I get back? What if I get back and there's nothing there?"

I knew I couldn't play the "what if" game in my head. You've been there, you've done that. You've heard that little voice in your head. And so my little first step was buy the plane ticket from Baltimore to Denver. And then I bought a ticket from Denver to San Francisco. And then I bought a ticket from San Francisco to Los Angeles. And from Los Angeles to Dallas. And from Dallas back home, right after the coolest Thanksgiving I ever had with the family of a friend in my entrepreneurial mastermind group.

Being able to generate that experience, though, wouldn't have happened unless I had looked at it and said "Okay, what's the smaller step here? What am I afraid of and how am I going to get over that?" I could have gone back to the Nike "Just do it, just buy the ticket." But that wouldn't have worked in my mind.

I would still have played that "what if" game of spending all that money, and coming back to having not earned all month.

But I did work a little bit on the road, and sure enough, when I got back and did the math, I had made the same amount of money while traveling and "not working", as I had the previous month.

This was my new reality. This was where my experience could overwrite the old one. As soon as I saw that and realized that the only fear that I really had, which was coming back to nothing, was gone, I did it again. December came around and I went on a three thousand mile road trip around the country.

So what I ask you is this: What is it that you really want to do? Is there something in your life, whether it's family, creativity, occupation, in whatever—is there something that you really want to achieve?

Maybe you want to write a book. Maybe you want to pick up public speaking and share your story?

Whatever it is, take that idea, break it down just like I did with the little twelve stairs. What are the parts that you need to do to see your dream come true?

What I want to leave you with is this: What is it that you really want to accomplish today? What is it that you put on your to-do list for tomorrow that's going to get pushed off to the next day and the next day, that's never going to get done? What can you identify and say "I'm gonna start right now"?

It's show time.

The Sequel

"Let today be the day you give up who you've been for who you can become."

–Hal Elrod

At this point in time, you are a clean slate. You are a new story ready to be born. Anything that you have labeled yourself as in the past whether it be failure or disappointment is in the past for a reason.

This is your fresh start and where you end up depends entirely on who you choose to be from this moment forward. It's not about what has happened in the past or the events that have occurred up until now. It's about who you want to be here and now in this moment. This is your moment.

Don't put off creating and experiencing life - happiness, health, wealth, success, and love - that you truly want and deserve for another day. As I always like to say, "There's nothing to it, but to do it!"

If you want your life to improve, you have to improve yourself first. Jump into the *Life Re-Scripted Inner Circle Community* today by visiting http://rescripted.life/bonus Then, without hesitation or excuses, commit to writing your new script tomorrow. You know, tomorrow, the day you begin your journey to re-writing the most extraordinary life story you have ever imagined.

If there is anything I can do to support you or add value to your life in any way, please let me know.

Contact Me Anytime

I'm always grateful to connect with like-minded individuals, and find it especially cool to hear from people who have read my book, seen my videos or attended my talks. So, if you have any questions or would just like to say hi, go to http://rescripted.life/contact and send me a message. I look forward to hearing from you, and exploring how I can add as much value to your life as I possibly can.

Let's Keep Sharing Our Gifts

May I ask you a quick favor?

If this book made a difference in your life, if you feel like your life has changed after reading it, and you see that living a Life Re-Scripted can be a new beginning for you to take any - or every - area of your life to the next level, I'm hoping you'll do something for someone you love:

Give this book to them. Let them borrow your copy. Ask them to read it. Or better yet, get them their own copy as a gift. The best gift you can give is the support to step into greatness.

Or it could be for no special reason at all, other than to say, "Hey, I love and appreciate you, and I want to help you live your best life. Read this."

If you believe, as I do that being a great friend or family member is about helping your friends and loved ones to become the best versions of themselves, I encourage you to share this book with them.

Please spread the word.

Thank you so much.

-Zephan

SPECIAL BONUS OFFER

<u>Your Free Gift</u>

As a way of saying thank you for purchasing this book, I'm offering you the following free book bonuses:

- The Life Re-Scripted Expert Interviews (over 40 entrepreneurs came together from all over the globe to share their secrets to creating a life and business on your own terms so that you can do it too)

- The Life Re-Scripted Transformation Challenge (to rewire your brain for maximum happiness and success so that you can discover your purpose and start living your dream life today)

- The Life Re-Scripted Inner Circle (a private community of entrepreneurs and life re-scripters from all over the globe who are living life on their own terms and want to support you because we all need someone to hold us accountable from time to time)

For exclusive access to these bonuses, go to

http://rescripted.life/bonus

Urgent Plea

Thank you for reading my book! This is the end (I promise) and I really appreciate all of your feedback. I love hearing what you have to say so feel free to reach out and contact me!

I need your input so that I can make my next book even better and to change more lives. Can I ask you to do something small for me?

Please leave me a helpful REVIEW on Amazon.

Thanks so much!!

~Zephan Moses Blaxberg

About The Author

Zephan Moses Blaxberg is the founder and host of the iTunes "New & Noteworthy" acclaimed Year Of Purpose Podcast where he interviews motivators and inspirational humans from all over the world who are living life on their own terms. He is one of the top authorities and mentors to those who are tired of living a mediocre life.

Zephan has held every job in the book from pastry chef to working at the Apple Store Genius Bar. He even founded a highly successful video production company landing him opportunities in the White House and on set for a Netflix Original Series. His videos can be seen in football stadiums and on major TV stations across the United States.

After realizing that there was more to life than settling for the script that had been handed down to him, he took a two month hiatus from life to couch-surf and travel hack his way around the country. When he got back the Year Of Purpose was born.

Since then he has dedicated his life to empowering others to discover what makes them tick and how they can lead a Life Re-Scripted.

Zephan now mentors his peers to discover their purpose in less time so that they can live the dream life they've always wanted.

www.ingramcontent.com/pod-product-compliance
Lightning Source LLC
Chambersburg PA
CBHW022039190326
41520CB00008B/646